R $2.95

ARCHITECTURE AND SCULPTURE IN IRELAND
1150-1350

ARCHITECTURE AND SCULPTURE IN IRELAND
1150-1350

R. A. Stalley

Gill and Macmillan . Dublin

Barnes & Noble Books . New York
A division of Harper & Row Publishers, Inc.

First published in 1971
Gill and Macmillan Ltd
2 Belvedere Place
Dublin 1
and in London through association with the
Macmillan
International Group of Publishing Companies
Published in the U.S.A. in 1972 by
Harper & Row Publishers, Inc.
Barnes & Noble Import Division

© R. A. Stalley 1971

Gill & Macmillan SBN: 7171 0555 5
Barnes & Noble ISBN: 06 4965007

Jacket design by Peter Wildbur
Typography and layout by Skehan Uhlemann

Printed and bound in the Republic of Ireland by
the Book Printing Division of
Smurfit Print and Packaging Limited, Dublin

CONTENTS

	Preface	vii
	Author's Preface	ix
1.	Introduction	1
2.	Patrons	7
3.	Craftsmen	17
4.	Castles	30
5.	Cathedrals	58
6.	Abbeys and Friaries	90
7.	Years of Decline	139
	Map	149

PREFACE

It gives me great pleasure to know that the Exhibition of Irish Architecture from 1150–1350 has been promoted by Rosc.

Irish architecture of this period has not had the attention of art historians to any degree. It could be because this period does not fit conveniently into the main definition of European architecture, either Romanesque or Gothic. It is generally thought that the great creative period in Ireland finished with the Norman invasion. This is not so, as any reader of this scholarly work will understand. In fact, stone architecture in a broader context did not exist before this period in Ireland, because it was only after this time that our larger cathedrals, churches and castles were built. The tragedy is that so little has survived.

Rosc is proud of this first publication under its inspiration.

MICHAEL SCOTT
Chairman of Rosc.

AUTHOR'S PREFACE

I hope this book will provide an introduction to a little known but fascinating period of Irish architecture and sculpture. I have not attempted to give a comprehensive survey; my aim has been to discuss works which are either outstanding in themselves or in some way representative. Inevitably the process of selection depended on personal choice, so the reader should not be disappointed if his favourite building or piece of sculpture has been omitted. At times the lack of suitable photographs forced me to limit discussion, and this was particularly so when talking of window tracery; for example, I could find no good photographs of the windows in the Dominican friary at Kilkenny. A further difficulty was the lack of detailed research on the period. One of the most important regional schools of Irish sculpture, which flourished in Connaught during the early years of the thirteenth century, has never received close analysis, and in many such areas I was forced to be tentative in my conclusions. I am only too aware that future research may well undermine much of what I have said.

I have naturally been dependent on the works of H. G. Leask, in particular his 'Irish Castles and Castellated Houses' (Dundalk 1941) and his three volumes on 'Irish Churches and Monastic Buildings' (Dundalk 1955–60). Equally important has been A. C. Champney's 'Irish Ecclesiastical Architecture' (London 1910); any reader seeking further information should refer to these authorities. For the history of the period I have used G. H. Orpen, 'Ireland under the Normans 1169–1333' (Oxford 1911–20), which contains many interesting references to architectural works, and A. J. Otway-Ruthven, 'A History of Medieval Ireland' (London 1968). Two primary sources yielded much information; these were the 'Calendar of Documents Relating to Ireland' edited by H. S. Sweetman (London 1875–86), and the Irish Pipe Rolls summarised in the Reports of the Deputy Keeper of the Public Records. For my chapters on 'Craftsmen' and 'Castles' I owe much to D. Knoop and G. P. Jones, 'The Medieval Mason' (Manchester 1933), and to the 'History of the King's Works' by R. Allen Brown, H. M. Colvin, and A. J. Taylor (London 1963).

I am grateful to Professor A. J. Otway-Ruthven, Miss A. O. Crookshank, and Mr R. J. Hill, all of whom took great trouble in reading the typescript and made many valuable suggestions. I owe much to

AUTHOR'S PREFACE

the discussions I had with Mr J. O'Callaghan and I must also thank my teachers at the Courtauld Institute, London, Professor G. Zarnecki, Dr P. Kidson and Mr C. Hohler, who introduced me to the subject of medieval art. The staff of the following libraries gave much helpful assistance: the Library, Trinity College, Dublin; the National Library of Ireland; the Library of the Royal Society of Antiquaries; and the Conway Library, the Courtauld Institute. I am also grateful to the secretarial staff in the Faculty of Arts office, Trinity College, in particular to Mrs S. Comiskey who spent many hours typing out my script at short notice.

The plans in the book were beautifully re-drawn by Mrs R. Moores from models kindly provided by the Commissioners of Public Works in Ireland. The plan of Dundrum Castle was based on the one in 'An Archaeological Survey of County Down', by kind permission of the Ministry of Finance, Government of Northern Ireland. Permission to reproduce photographs was given by the following: Commissioners of Public Works in Ireland: 2, 4, 5, 14, 15, 19, 21, 36, 40, 42, 44, 47, 48, 49, 51, 55, 58, 66; the Irish Tourist Board, Bord Fáilte: 12, 43, 72; the Courtauld Institute of Art, University of London: 1, 28, 32; J. K. St. Joseph, Cambridge University Collection: copyright reserved: 22, 63; the Ministry of Finance, Government of Northern Ireland: 13. All other photographs are by the author.

Trinity College, Dublin.
July 1971.

INTRODUCTION

CHAPTER 1

The visitor to Ireland cannot fail to be impressed by the splendour of the country's Georgian architecture, but few perhaps appreciate the equally fine achievements of the thirteenth century, a time of intense architectural activity, which has never received adequate recognition. This is partly because Irish medieval buildings have suffered more damage in the course of time than those elsewhere, the majority either destroyed or in ruins. Only a handful of medieval churches are still used for worship.

The two centuries from 1150 to 1350 form an exciting and distinct phase in Irish architectural history. The period opens with the spread of Cistercian monasteries, when a new concept of church architecture was first introduced into Ireland; it ends with the sharp decline in major building projects, which resulted from the economic and social troubles of the early fourteenth century. The period thus encompasses the most flourishing period of Anglo-Norman rule. This was an era of relative prosperity, a prosperity which is reflected in the architecture of the time.

A new concept of church architecture

The construction of large scale churches provided the medieval mason with his most complex and exacting tasks, and so church architecture naturally dominates any history of medieval building. It was during the twelfth century that major churches in stone were first constructed in Ireland. Although the preceding centuries had seen a marvellous flowering of the arts, relatively little concern had been shown towards architecture as such. Early Christian civilisation had placed far more emphasis on precious objects, such as croziers, shrines and intricately painted manuscripts, than it had on ambitious building projects. For a remarkably long period churches remained unsophisticated buildings, usually no more than simple rectangular chambers. Instead of one large church to accommodate sizeable congregations, the early monasteries consisted of a number of smaller buildings, entirely separate from each other. At Glendalough, for example, there are at least eight different churches scattered along the valley, all part of one monastic settlement.

During the twelfth century this approach to church architecture was surpassed by new and grander ideas introduced from abroad.

CHAPTER 1 INTRODUCTION

For the first time the basilican form was brought to Ireland: the concept of a church with a large central nave divided from adjoining aisles by piers or columns. The credit for inaugurating the change should go to St. Malachy of Armagh, who did so much to bring the Irish church more into line with the rest of Europe. Malachy had travelled in both France and Italy and he must have been impressed by the large churches then being constructed in the Romanesque style. On his return to Ireland in 1140 he organised the building of a new church at the monastery of Bangor. St. Bernard in his life of the Irish saint describes how 'it seemed good to Malachy that a stone oratory should be erected at Bangor like those which he had seen constructed in other regions. And when he began to lay the foundations, the natives wondered, because in that land no such buildings were to be found'. Although the church at Bangor has long since been destroyed, it is clear that it represented a radical departure from tradition.

Two years later in 1142 it was Malachy again who was responsible for bringing the first Cistercian monks to Ireland, and it was the Cistercians who consolidated the new approach to church architecture first expressed at Bangor. The order spread rapidly and their large if austere buildings must have appeared colossal to the native Irish. This movement towards grand churches on a vast scale received further impetus with the Anglo-Norman invasion of Ireland after 1169.

Between 1150 and 1200 the new ideas on church building existed alongside the more traditional approach, for native Irish monasteries continued to erect churches of diminutive size. These Irish monastic settlements, however, did not remain totally unaffected by foreign influence. Although their churches were still small, they were increasingly embellished with sculptural decoration, usually given the title 'Irish Romanesque'. A good example of this is the so-called 'Nun's Church' at Clonmacnoise finished in 1167 [Pl. 1, 2]. It consists of a simple rectangular nave and originally it had a small chancel attached to the east. Both the doorway and the chancel arch are lavishly carved with a wide range of ornamental motifs, part Irish and part English in origin. The carving tends to be exceptionally shallow, the designs barely incised in the stone, though when painted

INTRODUCTION   CHAPTER 1

[Pl. 1]
Clonmacnoise, Nun's Church (1167).

they would have been more prominent. The shallowness of Irish Romanesque carving is one of its most noticeable characteristics, almost as if it was carved by craftsmen used to painting and metalwork, rather than working with a chisel. Simple Romanesque churches such as those at Clonmacnoise continued to be erected until the end of the twelfth century. The cathedral at Ardmore built just before 1203, takes a similar form, which indicates how long the tradition persisted.

Secular architecture
Just as ideas on church building were transformed during the second half of the twelfth century, so too similar changes took place with regard to secular architecture. Before the invasion of 1169 large stone

CHAPTER 1 INTRODUCTION

[Pl. 2]
Clonmacnoise, Nun's Church,
detail of the chancel arch.

INTRODUCTION CHAPTER 1

houses were probably unknown in Ireland and the usual materials were either timber or wattle and daub. Even the Irish princes did not permit themselves dwelling places of stone, a fact which is vividly indicated by descriptions of a palace which was built for King Henry II outside the walls of Dublin in 1171. This we are told was 'a wonderful structure of wattle-work' erected at Henry's request in the native style by the Irish kings and chieftains who had submitted to him.

During the early years of the conquest, when they were deeply involved in war, the Anglo-Normans had neither the opportunity nor the resources to undertake major building projects in stone. Almost all their early castles took the form of motte and bailey fortifications, usually consisting of a huge mound of earth with timber defences on the top, encircled by a ditch below. But by the early years of the thirteenth century many of these wooden buildings were replaced in stone. Indeed the thirteenth century witnessed a tremendous expansion in the amount of stone building going on in Ireland. Massive castles such as those at Trim and Roscommon, stone houses in the cities, elaborate Gothic cathedrals such as those at Cashel or Kilkenny, the construction of city walls, and the erection of stone bridges over many of the rivers—all these were part of the great architectural achievement of the thirteenth century.

Destroyed buildings

One of the chief difficulties for the historian trying to plot the evolution of Irish medieval architecture is the destruction of some of the finest and probably most influential buildings. Malachy's church at Bangor has already been mentioned. Two of the most important Cistercian abbeys—Mellifont and St. Mary's, Dublin—are also largely destroyed, and one is left to guess the extent of their architectural influence. At Mellifont most of the foundations have been excavated, but at St. Mary's there is no trace of any of the buildings apart from the chapter house. A further gap is the cathedral of Armagh, totally reconstructed in the early nineteenth century, and perhaps a greater loss is St. Thomas' Abbey, Dublin, a large Augustinian house in the western suburbs of the medieval city. This was a royal foundation of 1177. Exactly fifty years later, a major reconstruction of the church was undertaken, King Henry III himself being invited to lay the first stone although in fact he was unable to

CHAPTER 1   INTRODUCTION

be present. In view of this royal patronage the abbey was almost certainly a lavish piece of work, but again we remain ignorant about its design. In secular architecture there are equally important gaps, the castle in Dublin being the most serious. As this was the seat of the royal administration, the design of its buildings would certainly have been up to date and no doubt set precedents for the rest of Ireland. This is especially true of the splendid hall constructed between 1243 and 1245 by order of Henry III, a design which no doubt reflected the latest architectural ideas at Westminster.

Despite these losses there remain many works of quality and interest, and although no Irish church can compare in scale with the vast Gothic cathedrals of England and the Continent, plenty of fine craftsmanship survives albeit at a more humble level. But before discussing the monuments themselves, it is necessary to look at the type of people responsible for creating them and the circumstances in which they lived.

PATRONS   CHAPTER 2

The Anglo-Normans

Apart from the arrival of the Cistercian monks, the major factor which determined the nature of Irish religious architecture was the Anglo-Norman invasion in the years after 1169. The conquest of Ireland was not so fast or efficiently organised as the Norman conquest of England a century before, but by 1250 about three-quarters of the country was under Anglo-Norman rule. In many ways the architectural results of the invasion were similar to those in England after the battle of Hastings. On both occasions, the conquest produced a wave of new religious foundations and led to the reconstruction of many existing cathedrals. In Ireland, as in England, the Normans were contemptuous of the type of churches they found and set about rebuilding them on a more ambitious and imposing scale. Christ Church, Dublin, Kildare, Ferns, Kilkenny are just a few of the cathedrals rebuilt through the initiative of Anglo-Norman ecclesiastics.

The career of John de Courcy provides a good example of the circumstances in which new monastic foundations took place. After his daring conquests in Ulster during 1177, he established a series of monastic houses in his recently acquired lands as part of the process of colonisation. At Inch, just outside Downpatrick, he founded a Cistercian monastery in 1180 [Pl. 3], and thirteen years later his wife, Affreca, founded another, Grey Abbey, in the Ards Peninsula. Benedictine monks from a monastery on John's family's estates in Somerset were also introduced and they established the priory of Ards. His other foundations included the Augustinian Priory of Toberglorie on the outskirts of Downpatrick. In addition to these religious benefactions, John de Courcy also carried out a great deal of building on his own account, constructing a series of castles in strategic positions to protect his new domains. Most of these were motte and bailey fortifications, but on the coast at Dundrum and Carrickfergus, parts of the stone castles are the result of his work [Pl. 4]. The number of buildings which resulted from John de Courcy's patronage was thus considerable, and in this respect he is typical of the Anglo-Norman leaders.

Religious endowments were a means of absolving the conscience, and were usually the product of sincere and genuine piety on the part of men like John de Courcy. Often there were special motives for

CHAPTER 2 PATRONS

[Pl. 3]
Inch Abbey, founded 1180 by John de Courcy. One of the earliest examples of Gothic architecture in Ireland.

PATRONS

CHAPTER 2

[Pl. 4]
Dundrum Castle; a castle was established on this site by John de Courcy and the inner bailey wall dates from his time.

CHAPTER 2 PATRONS

[Pl. 5]
Athassel Priory, tomb in the choir, probably commemorating Walter de Burgh who died in 1271.

such foundations. It is said that William Marshal established the abbey of Tintern as the result of a vow he had taken while in peril at sea, swearing to found an abbey in the place where he should ultimately land. The church at Tintern thus represents an act of personal thanksgiving.

Another consideration is that a monastery offered a place of retirement for many a Norman baron, a place of burial, a place where prayers would be said for him after his death. The vast Augustinian priory of Athassel in Tipperary served such purposes for the de Burgh family. Founded by William de Burgh at the end of the twelfth century, he and several of his descendants were buried in the abbey church, and the delicately carved though much battered tomb in the choir was almost certainly intended to commemorate one of them, probably Walter de Burgh who died in 1271 [Pl. 5, 6]. Only one panel of the tomb remains, divided into arches with tiny knights arranged beneath. The vigorous poses of the knights, especially the crossed

PATRONS

CHAPTER 2

[Pl. 6] Athassel Priory, detail from the tomb.

[Pl. 7]
Kilfane, tomb effigy, probably Thomas de Cantwell who died c. 1319.

PATRONS

CHAPTER 2

legs, are typical of English tomb sculpture in the second half of the thirteenth century and it has been suggested that it was imported ready carved from an English workshop. A large effigy of the deceased was once no doubt placed on the top. The finest such effigy to survive in Ireland is at Kilfane in Kilkenny where the huge figure of a knight complete with sword, shield and rowelled spurs is boldly depicted [Pl. 7]. This probably represents Thomas de Cantwell who died soon after 1319. The Cantwell family had settled in Kilkenny and Tipperary after the Norman conquest and owned property near Kilfane. The effigy, carved in Kilkenny marble, was made by a local craftsman who was clearly familiar with English conventions of the time, particularly evident in the crossed legs and the simple curving folds of the surcoat. The rigid pose and the awkward treatment of the arm betray the sculptor's inexperience, however. Nevertheless the carving provides a wonderful image of the type of person responsible for endowing many an Irish monastery in the middle ages.

Irish patrons

Benefactions were not restricted to Anglo-Norman patrons, for Irish leaders made similar endowments, both before and after the invasion. For example Cathal Crovderg O Conor, king of Connaught, 1202–24, founded Abbey Knockmoy for the Cistercians, and later in his life he also founded the Augustinian abbey of Ballintubber. But it was to Knockmoy that he returned when he withdrew from the turmoil of the world, for the Annals describe how he was there in 1224, when he died 'in the habit of a monk'.

The royal government

One of the most important results of the Anglo-Norman invasion was that it gave Ireland a centralised government for the first time in its history. This royal administration in Dublin had resources at its disposal which far surpassed those of any other patron, and expenditure on building occupied a significant proportion of the annual budget. This is primarily because castle building was an essential military activity and played a key rôle in the defence of newly conquered lands. In the years around 1280, for example, the government spent huge sums of money fortifying the castles of Athlone, Randown and Roscommon, in an effort to subdue the Irish of Connaught. But it was not just military works that the Crown financed. The royal

CHAPTER 2   PATRONS

foundation of St. Thomas' Abbey has been mentioned, and throughout the thirteenth century repeated donations, though small, were given to the Franciscan Friars, some of which must have been spent on their building projects. The most splendid piece of royal patronage, however, was the hall built in Dublin Castle by order of Henry III between 1243 and 1245. Henry was a king with more artistic than political wisdom and he gave very specific instructions about the design, commanding the justiciar and treasurer

> that out of the King's profits they cause to be constructed in the castle of Dublin, a hall 120 feet in length and 80 feet in breadth, with glazed windows after the hall of Canterbury; and that they cause to be made in the gable beyond the dais a round window 30 feet in diameter. They shall also cause to be painted beyond the dais the King and Queen seated with their baronage; and a great portal shall be made at the entrance to the hall.

There were some minor delays over construction but in 1245 Henry ordered the justiciar to finish it and link up the water supply. Inside, the hall was decorated with marble columns (which forty years later were appropriated by the bishop of Waterford) and in terms of style it seems to have represented the latest architectural fashions in the royal circle, particularly reflected in the use of marble shafts, and the introduction of the rose window.

The very detailed requirements of Henry, even down to the dimensions, provide a rare example of the way a patron might involve himself in building matters. But Henry is renowned for his artistic knowledge, and this type of concern was not so widespread among his nobles. Yet it does indicate the way patrons could influence the master mason in his designs. Normally, however, instructions were vague, a request to do something similar to a work seen elsewhere by the patron, just as Henry III referred to the hall of Canterbury. There was also no doubt a distinction between military and peacetime operations, for in the erection of the early motte and bailey castles, the Anglo-Norman leaders must have taken a directing hand. Hugh de Lacy appears to have been supervising the construction of a motte castle at Durrow in 1186, when he suffered the misfortune of being murdered by an Irishman with an axe.

PATRONS
CHAPTER 2

Regional nature of Irish architecture

It is unlikely that lay patrons exercised any influence over ecclesiastical designs except in an indirect way. At first sight it is tempting to attribute some of the stylistic traits common to the abbeys of Graiguenamanagh and Tintern, to the patronage of William Marshal, but such similarities are more conveniently explained by geographical proximity or the influence of a local school of masons. Indeed a prominent feature of Irish architecture in the period is the division into regional groups. In south Leinster for example the non-monastic churches of Thomastown, Gowran and the cathedral of Kilkenny have certain stylistic affinities, and another distinct group are those stark churches in the west of Ireland, characterised by plain pointed arches and thick unmoulded piers, such as are found in the Cistercian abbeys at Monasternenagh and Corcomroe, or the cathedral of Limerick. Some of these regional groups can be explained by the distinction between Anglo-Norman and Irish patronage, and this provides one of the most intriguing themes of Irish architectural history in the Middle Ages. For example in the early decades of the thirteenth century it is clear that one particular band of sculptors worked at Boyle, Cong, Knockmoy and Inishmaine, but they do not appear to have gone outside Connaught to work under the Anglo-Normans. However, it would be wrong to suppose that architectural ideas did not at times transcend this political division. The master masons who designed the church at Boyle, a Cistercian abbey in county Roscommon remote from English influence, seem to have been aware of the latest styles of architecture current in the west of England. Nevertheless Boyle is an exceptional building, and in general those parts of Ireland furthest from Anglo-Norman influence tend to display a more local form of architecture.

Sources of finance

Although lay patrons had little influence over the actual design of churches, it was they who were ultimately responsible for financing building work, since they provided the landed endowment from which most religious organisations received their income. Normally any building enterprise had to be paid for out of these established revenues, which were chiefly derived from the land. Occasionally there were supplementary sources of money, and the Deeds of Christ Church Cathedral provide some interesting examples. In 1289 the bishop of Ferns granted an indulgence to those 'who by legacy or

CHAPTER 2   PATRONS

gift promote the building of Holy Trinity Church'. Such indulgences were a common medieval device for encouraging donations towards building projects. However, gifts did not always have to be contrived in this way, and some churches could expect substantial voluntary contributions. In about 1216 a certain Philip Portbich granted to Christ Church some land and 'ten shillings and ten sheep towards the building of the church; also one cow and one heifer, and during his life a sheep at the Nativity of St. John the Baptist'. A few years later in 1225 the neighbouring cathedral of St. Patrick adopted a more positive approach to augmenting their income by acquiring official protection for four years for 'preachers of the fabric' going through Ireland to beg alms. But despite these additions, most expenditure on building had to be met out of the normal revenues derived from land, and in the case of many of the smaller monasteries it is unlikely that they were in a position to resort to any other means. In general the income of Irish churches was very much lower than their English counterparts. The annual total of rents and profits coming to the abbot of Inch in the years around 1302–6 was a mere £10 19s 4d, a contrast to the seemingly immense revenue of the mother house at Furness in Lancashire whose temporalities were worth £176 in 1292. Although Inch was a small house there were few Irish monasteries with an income above £50 per year. Inevitably this poverty allowed for little investment in building. It explains why Irish abbey churches tend to be small in scale, and it also led to very slow progress when building work was undertaken. With so little to spend, it took many years for churches to be completed. Boyle Abbey was begun soon after 1161, but the church cannot have been finished much before 1230, to judge from the style of the west end. Even the cathedrals were in no better financial position, and the relative wealth of Christ Church, Dublin only served to emphasise the difficulties of many others.

CRAFTSMEN CHAPTER 3

Any major architectural project demands elaborate organisation, and sufficient records survive from the thirteenth century to give an indication of the way works were carried out at the time. One of the most fascinating pieces of evidence is a short building account for repairs to the royal castles of Dundrum and Greencastle in 1260. The man in charge was Robert Gelus and the account lists the precise sums to be spent on various items. For Greencastle he had to buy a variety of timber, joists, planks, poles and boards for making a wooden gallery, and he also had to pay for transporting the timber out of the woods. Then there are payments to carpenters working on the roof of the hall of the castle and it was probably for the roof that he spent £2 8s 4d on twenty-six feet of lead purchased at Drogheda. Some stone building was going on at the same time and there are a series of entries in connection with this. He had to pay stone cutters working in a quarry, and then purchase forty crannocks of lime at Carlingford as well as provide for its carriage to Greencastle. In addition to the lime, water and sand were needed for mixing mortar and these had to be brought up from the seashore, labourers receiving payment for carrying it. There are similar entries for work on the gateway at Dundrum, and these include the purchase of free-stone at Down, as well as payments to masons for laying it in place. Robert Gelus also had to buy iron at Drogheda for repairing the actual doors, as well as paying workmen for forging it. The account thus provides a remarkable illustration of the type of activities which building operations required.

Royal works

The official capacity of Robert Gelus is unknown. In most medieval building projects strictly administrative tasks of this sort were not necessarily performed by a person involved in the technical problems of construction. In the royal works it was normal for either the constable of the castle concerned or the local sheriff to supervise minor tasks, but by the thirteenth century major operations had a separate official appointed as 'keeper of the works'. Thus during the reconstruction of Roscommon Castle 1280–5, Gregory de Coquile is cited as 'Keeper of the Works of the Castle of Roscommon'. Dublin Castle appears to have had a semi-permanent keeper of the works by this time, an office which Thomas Burel, described as 'a citizen of

CHAPTER 3 CRAFTSMEN

Dublin', filled between 1279 and 1285. The job usually involved recruiting workmen, purchasing materials, arranging their transportation to the site, and organising the financial side of things. To what extent such men determined architectural design is never easy to say. They must have exercised a general control over it and some may have been involved in the details, but the actual job of construction was probably left to a master mason on the site.

When King John came to Ireland in 1210 he brought with him a group of craftsmen who travelled in his entourage. There was Nicholas the carpenter, Osbert the quarrier, Alberic the ditcher, Pinell the miner, and Urricus the engineer. The latter was noted as a builder of siege engines, a function he had exercised for the Crown in England as early as 1193–4. These specialist craftsmen were clearly brought to supervise urgent operations on royal castles, no doubt directing the labour of local workmen. The need for John to bring his own men suggests that at this stage there was no body of craftsmen permanently employed by the royal government in Dublin. However, later in the century the situation had changed, as is suggested by the appointment in 1284 of William de Prene as 'Carpenter of the King's Houses and Castles in Ireland'. He was given a shilling a day for his sustenance and forty shillings a year for his robes. There is no evidence to indicate whether there was a corresponding master mason and it is probable that William de Prene, although a carpenter, was the sole directing mind over royal building since he was described in 1290 as 'Keeper of the King's Works in Ireland'. His appointment, especially seen alongside Thomas Burel's post at Dublin Castle, implies that by the end of the thirteenth century the royal works in Ireland were being more coherently organised and that a permanent group of skilled men in the pay of the Crown was gradually being formed. The career of William de Prene also shows that successful craftsmen could rise to the top administrative positions, and that the distinction between administrative and technical affairs was no fixed barrier.

William de Prene
In the years after 1284, William de Prene can be traced working at both Athlone and Roscommon Castles, and he received considerable grants of land as a reward for his endeavours. But in 1292 his successful career was abruptly halted when he was arrested on a long list of

CRAFTSMEN

CHAPTER 3

charges. These included stealing sixty shillings worth of nails from Roscommon Castle and selling them in Dublin, taking twenty pounds in wages due to other carpenters at the castle, embezzling three hundred pounds by falsifying the accounts of workmen he employed, and a more technical charge of 'faulty work'. This latter concerned the collapse of a bridge at Limerick as a result of which eighty men had been drowned. William de Prene was eventually found guilty of most of the charges. He was dismissed from the King's service, his property was confiscated and he was flung in prison until he could find pledges worth two hundred pounds. In subsequent records he is ignominiously described as a felon, and by 1293 his job had been taken over by Adam de Claverle. The case ironically illustrates the responsibilities of the top architectural jobs. It shows the large sums of money involved and the way officials had to take responsibility for the quality of the work under their control. Disasters such as that at Limerick were not as rare as one might imagine. In 1211, for example, a newly constructed tower at Athlone collapsed and on this occasion nine men were killed. It seems that the tower had been erected on a mound of earth which had not fully settled.

Religious building
There is far less evidence about ecclesiastical building, although some of the arrangements were probably similar to those in the royal works. In England a 'keeper of the fabric' was often appointed and, where a cathedral was concerned, this might be one of the canons. Again the same problem arises as to the extent to which such officials were involved in design. Elias of Dereham, a canon of Salisbury was director of the fabric there in the early thirteenth century, and he was elsewhere described as an 'incomparabilis artifex'. But on most occasions the process of design must have been left to a professional master mason brought in from outside, as appears to have been the case for the building of the nave of Christ Church, Dublin. One Irish ecclesiastic who did get involved in building operations was Master Maurice Jak, precentor of Kildare Cathedral. He is said to have constructed a bridge across the river Liffey at Kilcullen in 1319 and another across the river Barrow at Leighlin, some parts of which still survive. It is not unlikely that Maurice Jak first got involved in this type of work in an official capacity such as 'keeper of the fabric' in his own cathedral.

CHAPTER 3   CRAFTSMEN

The procedure in Cistercian abbeys seems to have been rather different. The famous statement by Ordericus Vitalis that 'all Cistercian monasteries are constructed in deserts and in the middle of woods, and the monks build them with their own hands' needs qualification, but there is some truth in it. The construction of the first Cistercian house in Ireland, at Mellifont, was supervised by a monk, Robert, sent over from France, and since manual labour formed an essential part of the Cistercian way of life, the monks themselves must always have been involved in building. This was certainly the case at Boyle where the death of Donnsleibhe O hInmhainén, 'a holy monk and chief master of the carpenters' is recorded in 1230. Cistercian monasteries generally had a large proportion of lay brothers attached to them, and they performed the more mundane tasks of life. These no doubt included labouring on any building works currently being undertaken. At times, however, outside workmen were brought in. It seems certain that Boyle had professional master masons in charge, mainly because decisive changes of style in the church imply the presence of different personalities, all of whom were well informed about architecture in the west of England. If the monks had been in control, it is likely that the style would have been more local in flavour and more consistent throughout the church. Indeed the west window is so close to work at Christ Church, Dublin that the Christ Church master may have been called in to design it.

Foreign masons

After the Anglo-Norman invasion, it is clear that a considerable number of English craftsmen found their way to Ireland. In the first half of the thirteenth century, for example, a certain Nicholas of Coventry described as 'cementarius' was working in Dublin, and no doubt there were several others like him in the city. One of these was the master mason who designed the nave of Christ Church Cathedral. Although his name is unknown, it is possible to deduce quite a lot about him. Earlier in his career he was employed in Worcestershire, where he was involved in the construction of churches. Sometime about 1190–1200 he worked on the north transept of St. Andrew's, Droitwich, and here he carved some capitals which have similarities to those found in the cathedral at Dublin [Pl. 8]. These consist of heads projecting from a background of foliage. The shape of the heads, the curls of the hair, and the fondness for carving faces with grimacing

CRAFTSMEN CHAPTER 3

[Pl. 8]
St. Andrew's, Droitwich, capitals
in the north transept
(c. 1190–1200).

CHAPTER 3   CRAFTSMEN

[Pl. 9]
St. Faith's, Overbury, capital in the chancel (c. 1200).

expressions indicate that the same hand was at work in both places [Pl. 10, Pl. 29]. The Droitwich sculpture is, however, an earlier work since the style is not so evolved as at Dublin. A few years later, this particular mason worked on a second Worcestershire church in the village of Overbury at the foot of the Bredon Hills [Pl. 9]. Here the characteristics of his style re-appear in the chancel, though it is now more developed, as can be seen from the carving of the foliage. Certain architectural details at Overbury are identical to ones found in Christ Church and indicate that this mason was not just employed on sculpture but was controlling all aspects of the building. There was,

CRAFTSMEN
CHAPTER 3

[Pl. 10]
Christ Church Cathedral, Dublin,
capitals in the nave (c. 1220).

of course, no distinction between the sculptural and the purely architectural aspects of a master mason's work. Some time about 1213 this Worcestershire craftsman was brought to Ireland to work on Christ Church Cathedral. Why he in particular was selected and how the cathedral authorities knew about his work is not known. But there can be no doubt that it was he who designed the splendid elevation of the nave, and carved the fine capitals which decorate it.

Labour and materials
The career of the Christ Church master emphasises the basically itinerant nature of the life of a medieval mason, ready to travel

CHAPTER 3 CRAFTSMEN

wherever he could find work. In the Irish records there are several references to craftsmen moving from one job to another, and it appears that the employer had to pay the travelling expenses. In 1284 for example twelve masons who had journeyed to Roscommon were allowed a shilling each. The recruiting of workmen was obviously one of the first major tasks for anyone embarking on a building project. Another was the provision of materials, particularly stone and timber. For the stone a suitable quarry had to be found, and arrangements made for transporting it to the site. A recent article by D. M. Waterman* has proved that a large number of thirteenth century buildings in the south and east of Ireland used stone brought from a quarry at Dundry just outside Bristol. Clearly the Dundry quarry was a flourishing business since it provided material for many English works as well as ones in Ireland. An insight into the trade is provided by an incident which took place in 1251, when the royal bailiffs at Bristol, needing to repair the local castle, seized some stone which was awaiting shipment to St. Thomas' Abbey, Dublin. Not surprisingly, their action evidently provoked a strong protest from the canons. Christ Church Cathedral also used imported stone, both from Dundry and from the Isle of Purbeck in Dorset. Stone from the latter quarry was used for the black marble shafts which decorate the windows and the triforium in the cathedral, and the stone appears to have been pre-cut into cylindrical form, each shaft sixteen and a quarter inches long. The use of imported stone is not as surprising as it might seem initially. Carriage over land presented great difficulties and water transport was a much easier method. Even so, transport costs represented a considerable proportion of any building expenditure. At Athlone in 1233, of eighty marks needed for finishing the bridge, thirty were spent on the carriage of materials.

The provision of timber was probably not so difficult, but it still had to be selected and cut. The Pipe Roll of 1211–12 records a payment of 6s 8d to a carpenter sent, presumably from Dublin, into Munster to look for timber, and it seems surprising that it was necessary to go so far afield. Other materials like sand and lime could no doubt be found closer at hand, but if the building was in a remote

*'Somersetshire and other Foreign Building Stone in Medieval Ireland, c. 1175–1400', Ulster Journal of Archaeology, Volume 33, 1970.

CRAFTSMEN

CHAPTER 3

area, items such as iron, lead, nails, might have to be brought some distance.

Finance and weather

With materials and workmen assembled then came the problems of supervision and payment. The usual rate of pay for a mason in England up until the Black Death was four pence a day and from the little evidence available it appears the same rate applied in Ireland. The number of masons employed depended on the season of the year. As today, the summer months were best for building. During the winter, work occasionally stopped altogether, as happened during the construction of the hall at Dublin Castle in 1244. On 12 January the King sent an order urging the Treasurer that work completed so far should 'be well covered in, so that it may not be damaged by the intemperance of the weather'. In this case, however, lack of finance may have contributed to the halt in operations. Indeed progress was always closely dictated by the money available. Where finance was insufficient, loans must have played a part, particularly in urgent royal works. This was apparently the case in 1275–6 when forty pounds were repaid to Hugh of Lucca, an Italian merchant, who had lent the money to the justiciar to 'fortify the castle of Roscommon'. There is no evidence to show whether religious houses resorted to loans to finance construction.

Interruptions

Apart from bad weather and lack of money, there were other factors which could interfere with progress. In 1233 work on the bridge at Athlone was considered more urgent than masonry work at Randown Castle, so the King ordered work at Randown to cease and the money to be transferred accordingly. But the most dangerous interruptions were likely to come from the depredations of war. While work was in progress at Boyle Abbey in 1202, Cathal Crovderg O Conor and William de Burgh with their armies took over the monastery. The Annals of Loch Cé describe events with a sense of outrage, and state that 'no structure in the monastery was left without breaking and burning, except the roofs of the houses alone; and even of these a great portion was broken and burned'. The account then explains how a stone wall was built in a mere two days around the hall of the guests, presumably to fortify it. The speed of this operation implies

CHAPTER 3 CRAFTSMEN

that there was stone lying ready for use, no doubt intended for monastic building. After the departure of the unwanted visitors, the monks must have had to devote their energies to repairing the damage, inevitably halting work on the church. It seems therefore that building in Ireland during the early Middle Ages was a spasmodic process, dependent on the fortunes of money, politics and weather, and, even at the best of times, progress was inordinately slow by modern standards. Only the Crown had sufficient resources to build quickly, as at Roscommon, for example, where the castle appears to have been totally rebuilt in the relatively short time of five years.

Castles and churches

Although castles and churches are usually considered separately in the history of architecture, it is worth remembering that the same types of craftsmen were employed on both. The construction of a castle was infinitely less complex than the intricate work on a large church, but there were times when the masons employed were allowed to show their skill. At Athenry there is a series of finely carved capitals, and at Ferns a neatly designed chapel is fitted into one of the towers. This is roofed by an elaborate rib vault complete with carved bosses, and the corbels on which the ribs rest have capitals so precisely executed that they more than equal their counterparts in ecclesiastical architecture [Pl. 11].

Bridges and houses

In addition to castles and churches, masons were also employed on bridges and houses, though few remnants of this work survive. Ireland appears to have had several bridges which were defended by towers at one end, like those still surviving at Monmouth in England and Cahors in France. The bridge at Dublin took this form; so too did those at Limerick and Galway, as well as the vitally strategic bridge over the Shannon at Athlone.

By the end of the thirteenth century, a number of stone houses had begun to appear, at least in Dublin. Although the very reference to them in surviving records is usually interpreted as proof of their rarity, there were enough to receive regular mention. As early as 1234, a certain Geoffrey de Lyvet owned a 'great stone hall', and by 1312 Geoffrey de Morton, a former mayor and chamberlain of Dublin, had

CRAFTSMEN CHAPTER 3

[Pl. 11]
Ferns Castle
one of the corbels
in the chapel
(second half
13th century).

CHAPTER 3   CRAFTSMEN

built a hall, presumably of stone, against the city wall. As he had narrowed the wall in order to get more space for himself and had blocked the passage along the top, he was brought to account by the authorities and required to amend the situation. Morton also built a series of embattled houses overlooking the wall, and these must have been of stone for defensive reasons.

Urban defence

The Morton case demonstrates the concern felt for the protection of the city, a concern which naturally increased as urban life expanded during the thirteenth century. A wall enclosing Dublin was started between 1204 and 1221, and this was fortified at certain points by flanking towers. Among the other places which took active measures for their defence was the flourishing town of New Ross. The construction of the walls in 1265 occurred in dramatic circumstances, for the townsfolk feared they might suffer harm from the current feud between Maurice Fitz Maurice and Walter de Burgh. An old Norman-French poem describes how the fortifications were constructed. A meeting of the principal men of the town and the commonalty was held where it was decided to erect 'a wall of mortar and stone'. The poem describes how the line of the ditch was marked out, and labourers hired to start work. Since the project was desperately urgent, the labourers were assisted by the townsfolk themselves, each of the various tradesmen giving a day's work. Eventually the poem triumphantly states that 'when the town shall be enclosed, and the wall completely fortified, no one in Ireland will be so hardy as to attack them in full view'. The co-operation of the townsfolk was probably a rare occurrence, caused only by the immediacy of the danger confronting them, and for the most part the city and town walls of Ireland must have been built by hired labourers. Relatively few highly skilled masons would have been needed, since the construction of such walls and towers did not involve problems of much complexity. But although such enterprises were not as sophisticated as the building of churches or castles, they nevertheless must have made a strong visual impact on the landscape of Ireland, an impact which has now been largely effaced by the expansion of towns and cities beyond their former boundaries. The most magnificent remnant to survive is the huge double-towered gateway at Drogheda, known as St. Lawrence's Gate [Pl. 12]. Constructed during the middle of the

thirteenth century, it is as strong as the gateway to any contemporary fortress, and provides a powerful testimony of the strength of the city's medieval defences.

[Pl. 12]
Drogheda, St. Lawrence's Gate, the finest town gateway to survive in Ireland.

CHAPTER 4 CASTLES

The idea of the castle, in the generally accepted sense of the word, was almost unknown in Ireland before the arrival of the Anglo-Normans in 1169. In England the castle had already seen over a hundred years of development, and this technical knowledge gave the invaders a decisive military advantage. By now the majority of English castles were built of stone, but these took too long to construct to be of any use in the early years of an invasion. Consequently the Anglo-Normans resorted to the motte and bailey fortification which had served them so well in their conquest of England a hundred years before. Provided a large force was available, a motte and bailey castle could be constructed with great speed, since the main task involved shifting huge quantities of earth, which did not demand skilled labour. The only skilled craftsmen needed were carpenters to construct the wooden buildings and palisades usually erected on the mound. Thus the invaders quickly provided themselves with a safe refuge in hostile territory. The impressive remains of these Norman earthworks are a prominent feature of the Irish countryside, and they are thickly scattered in areas where the Anglo-Norman settlement was intense.

The first castle at Trim
The motte and bailey castle was essentially a temporary building, which had difficulty in withstanding a long and sustained siege. The first castle at Trim, erected about 1172, evidently took this form, since the Song of Dermot describes how Hugh de Lacy 'fortified a house at Trim, and threw a ditch around it, and then enclosed it with a palisade'. However, the following year the warden of the castle felt too insecure to repulse an attack from Rory O'Connor and fled before the Irish prince arrived. The song states that the Irish 'threw down the mote and levelled it even with the ground, but first of all they put the house to flames'. After this sort of experience, the Anglo-Normans were clearly eager to reconstruct their more strategic castles in stone, as soon as they had the chance. This vastly increased the building's defensive strength and guarded against the dangers of fire.

CASTLES   CHAPTER 4

Carrickfergus

One of the most common forms of stone castle in England during this period was the great rectangular keep surrounded by a curtain wall. At the time of the invasion of Ireland, King Henry II himself was spending over five thousand pounds on the construction of such a castle at Dover to guard the crucial crossing of the English Channel, and in Ireland the Anglo-Normans constructed several castles of this type. The best preserved is at Carrickfergus, where the castle is set on a rocky promontory on the shore of Belfast Lough. Here the massive square keep, 90 feet high, survives almost intact. There are four storeys altogether, and the great chamber on the second floor provides the finest example in Ireland of an interior room in an Anglo-Norman castle [Pl. 13]. The dividing arch in the centre is a later addition, although similar dividing walls can be found in many keeps of this

[Pl. 13] Carrickfergus Castle; the great chamber on the second floor of the keep. (c. 1200).

CHAPTER 4 CASTLES

date. Carrickfergus was begun by John de Courcy, but the keep may not have been finished when he met his downfall in 1204. However, there is little doubt that the inner bailey wall, which was built before the keep, was erected through his initiative.

The remains of another square keep exist at the much neglected castle at Adare. It stands inside the inner bailey which is surrounded by a deep ditch, still retaining water. The outer bailey, flanked on one side by the river Maigue, contains the remnants of several buildings, including the remains of two halls.

Trim

By far the most intriguing and unorthodox version of the square keep can be found at the spectacular castle of Trim [Plan 1], which presents the architectural historian with three difficult problems. First, there is the question of its date. After the destruction of the motte and bailey castle in 1173, a replacement was soon built, but again this appears to have been a timber building. However, in view of the previous disaster one suspects an early attempt would have been made to reconstruct it in stone. The design of the present keep suggests it was

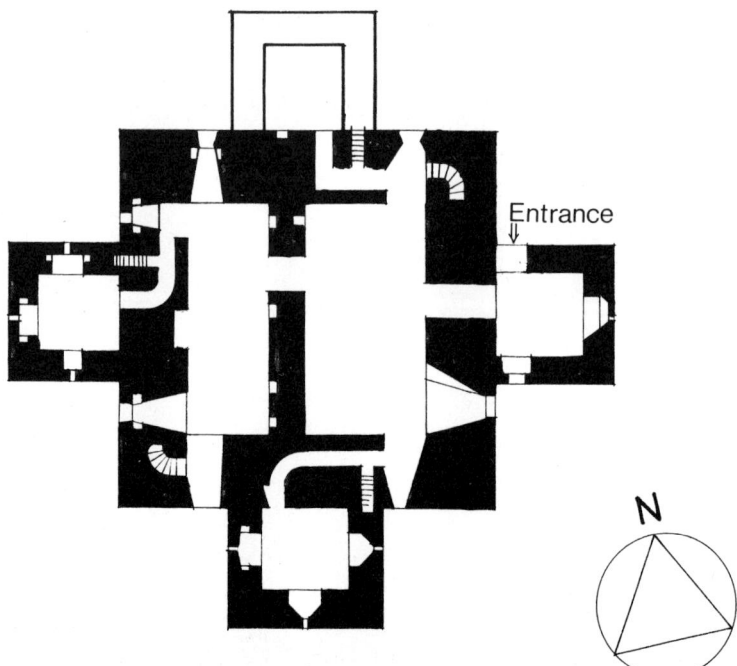

1 Trim Castle (keep)

CASTLES   CHAPTER 4

built about 1190–1200, but the documentary evidence implies a rather later date. When King John stayed at Trim in 1210, the castle was apparently too small to accommodate his court for his writs are dated from a meadow nearby. This suggests the keep was not yet finished, and probably not even begun. Two years later, in 1212, twenty-two shillings were paid for a large cable 'for demolishing the tower', presumably the old wooden tower which was now about to be replaced. In the same year over fifty four pounds were spent on the works of the castle, and clearly Trim was the centre of much activity at this time. This therefore seems the likely date for the start of the keep. Eight years later in 1220 the Annals of Innisfallen briefly state 'the castle of Trim was built by William Peppard, Lord of Tabor', a statement which is hard to believe. William Peppard does not appear to have had any connection with Trim, and his name could be a mistake for William de Lacy who was looking after Meath from 1215 to 1220. However, the reference in the Annals may indicate that the keep was now finished. If so, it was constructed in the eight years from 1212 to 1220, about the time needed for such a building.

This leads us on to the second problem, namely, for whom was the keep built? From about 1194 until his death in 1241 Walter de Lacy was Lord of Meath, and as Trim was the head of the lordship, he is the most likely candidate. But at the very period when work was apparently begun, the castle had been confiscated by the Crown. It was taken by John in 1210 and not returned until 1215. Thus it appears that the keep was started by the Crown, and finished by the de Lacy family after they regained control.

However, if Trim was started as a royal building, the choice of design was extremely odd [Pl. 14]. One would expect the Crown to be aware of the latest ideas on castle-building, but the plan of Trim is outmoded for the date. It is a variant of the normal keep of this type, for the square nucleus has a side chamber added on each face. These give the keep an exciting and unusual appearance, but although neat in plan, they form a severe military weakness. Their walls are thin in contrast to the main walls of the keep—in fact extraordinarily thin in those parts with internal staircases—and, more important, they greatly add to the number of vulnerable corners which the building presented to any attacker. Corners were relatively easy to undermine, since the

CHAPTER 4 CASTLES

[Pl. 14]
Trim Castle, the square projections on each face give it an unorthodox appearance; the west projection has been destroyed.

CASTLES CHAPTER 4

enemy could knock out the angle stones, and when sufficient had been removed, the walls above would collapse. So the fewer sharp angles a building contained, the better. By 1200 this was becoming generally realised and circular walls which avoided angles altogether were increasingly employed. But the architect of Trim was either oblivious of the dangers or else ignored them. Perhaps Irish siege warfare was sufficiently crude to encourage complacency, but it is worth remembering that it was through undermining one of the angle towers that King John brought down the walls of Rochester keep in 1215. The point of the design at Trim is not easy to fathom. The side chambers may have been intended to give flanking fire to the main angles of the keep, but more probably they were a rather hazardous device for increasing the number of rooms inside. The plan occurs only once elsewhere in the period, at Castle Rushen in the Isle of Man, where the side chambers were an addition to a square keep. The unpopularity of the scheme suggests that its faults were soon realised.

Although the main walls at Trim are eleven feet thick, it is noticeable that no rooms were constructed in the thickness of the wall, as was common in many English keeps. At Dover for example the immense walls are a maze of passages and rooms, but at Trim they contain only staircases. It was probably to compensate for this lack of mural space that the architect decided to add the four separate projecting chambers.

In other ways, however, Trim follows the pattern of the twelfth century keeps in England. For example, the cross wall which divides it into two halves is found regularly, so too is the combination of entrance and chapel in a forebuilding to the east, the entrance on the first floor, the chapel in the corresponding space above. At Trim this forms one of the four projecting chambers, but normally it was the only building added to the side of the keep. Whoever designed Trim was thus familiar with the design of English castles yet apparently unaware of or uninterested in the latest tactical considerations.

The date, the patron, and the design, therefore, all present historical problems for which there is no easy solution. One possible explanation which could solve the difficulties is that building operations extended over a very long period. The keep might have been started in the

CHAPTER 4 CASTLES

1190's by Walter de Lacy, but not finished until 1220. This would account for its outmoded design, though it would indicate that the tower demolished in 1212 was not on the site of the present keep. However, the suggestion is no more than hypothesis, and perhaps one should admit that the mysteries of Trim still remain to be solved.

As Trim was the head of the lordship of Meath, the castle was an important administrative centre and probably had a permanent staff of officials. To serve their needs, other buildings were required besides the keep—stables and storehouses for example. The majority of these were no doubt made of wood, but the remains of some stone ones can be seen on the north side of the bailey. A few of these outbuildings are mentioned in a royal mandate of 1224 which gave Walter de Lacy permission to take over 'the hall, houses and chambers in the castle of Trim' so that he and his retinue might dwell there when fighting both his own and the King's enemies. This comment is valuable in providing a brief glimpse of the size of the establishment at the castle.

The outer defences of Trim
Indeed the bailey at Trim is particularly large, over three acres in area, and the whole of this was enclosed by a curtain wall with the river and moat beyond forming the outer defences [Plan 2]. The design of the curtain wall indicates that it was built after the keep was finished. Projecting half round towers are placed at intervals along the south and east sections and such towers only came into fashion towards the middle of the thirteenth century. Apart from the timber palisades of motte and bailey castles, the earliest curtain walls in Ireland were usually plain. At Dundrum and Carrickfergus, for example, the inner bailey walls constructed by John de Courcy before 1200 took this form. The next stage in the development is illustrated by the middle curtain at Carrickfergus, built about 1200. This is fortified by one polygonal and two square towers, so arranged as to give covering arrow fire along the wall, either from slits in the towers or from battlements at the top. Such flanking towers had already been employed in England and the Continent, and at Dover (1168–90), no less than fourteen were arranged systematically along the wall.

About the turn of the century, there was a further technological advance. Just as square keeps were going out of fashion on account of

CASTLES

CHAPTER 4

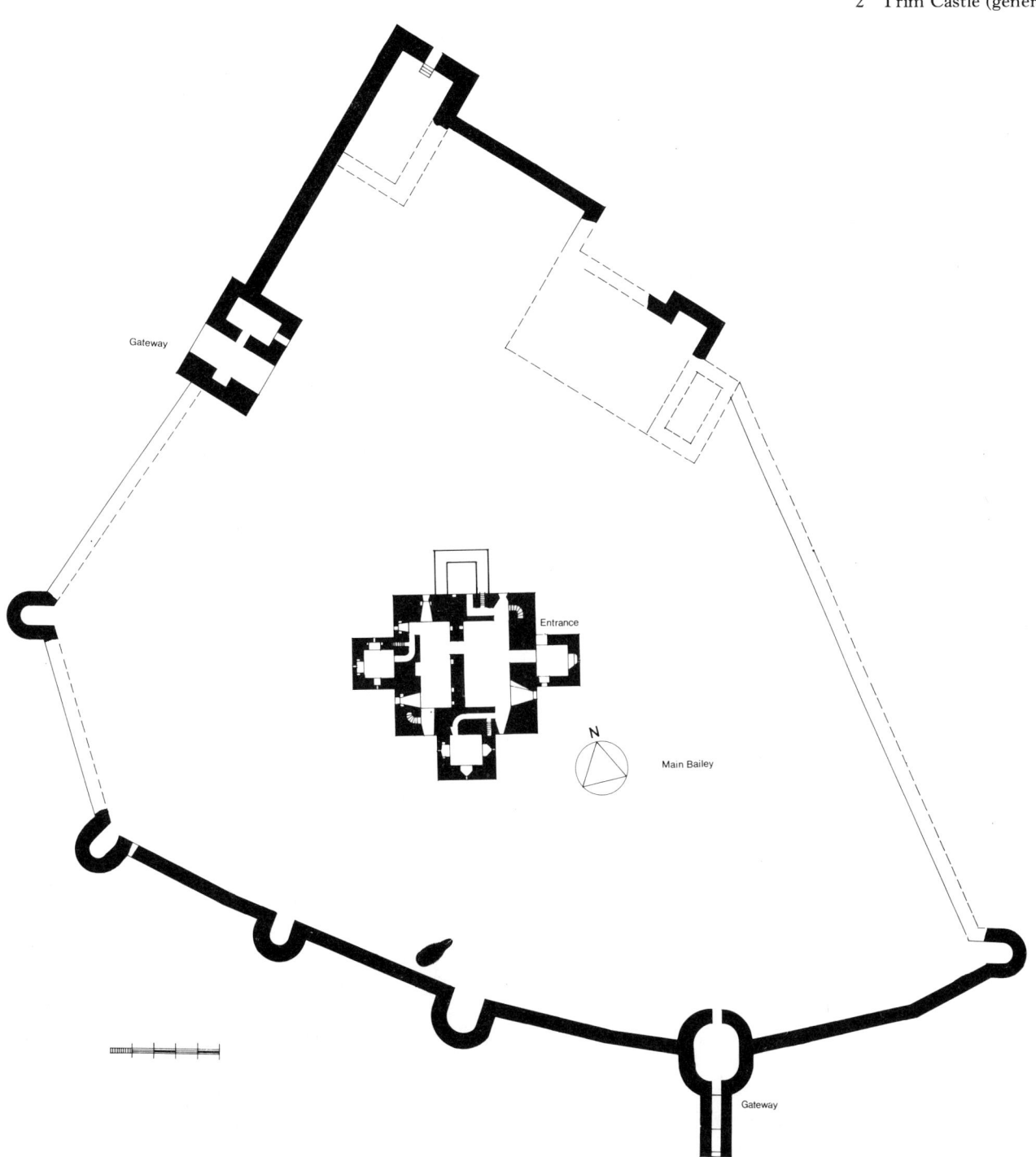

2   Trim Castle (general layout)

37

CHAPTER 4   CASTLES

their vulnerable corners, so too were square flanking towers whose angles were similarly exposed to the risks of picking and sapping. Thus the half circular or 'D' tower was introduced to overcome the danger. They are found as early as 1197–8 in the celebrated castle that Richard I built at Chateau Gaillard, high on a rock above the river Seine in Normandy. Shortly afterwards similar towers were incorporated in the outer wall at Dover. These were both royal castles, and it was some time before the method became widespread. Flanking 'D' towers are, however, found on the middle curtain wall at Chepstow, evidently built by William Marshal between 1189 and 1219. In Ireland the curtain walls at Trim erected after 1220 must represent one of the earliest uses of the technique.

Powerful curtain walls would have been of no value unless the gateways through them were equally well defended. They were the weakest point of the castle and a great deal of thought was given to them by military architects. During the twelfth century and after, one of the most common forms consisted of a square tower with a passage beneath, usually defended by a drawbridge over the moat in front, and by a portcullis fitted in the passageway. By the early years of the thirteenth century a barbican was sometimes added to give further protection. At Trim both entrances are furnished with them and here they consisted of walled passageways, extending out beyond the main gates. This meant that in order to reach the gates, the enemy had to force their way through the narrow passage of the barbican where they could be easily obstructed and attacked. The south gate at Trim is a sophisticated design in this respect [Pl. 15]; it is both neat and effective. A circular tower commands the curtain wall and it is pierced by the entrance passage below. This is continued out over the moat by two walls before reaching the turret of the barbican. A drawbridge was fitted inside the walls, and above there was a chamber provided with arrow slits from which to attack the enemy on both sides. The design is unique in Ireland and for parallels one has to look to England. One of the closest is the Black Gate at Newcastle, though this is rather more elaborate. Here the passage passes through a circular tower forming half-moon shaped guard rooms on either side, as is the case at Trim. The Black Gate was erected about 1247–50, but the Trim gate may be slightly earlier, since it appears to be contemporary with the adjoining curtain wall.

CASTLES CHAPTER 4

[Pl. 15]
Trim Castle, the south gate-tower and barbican.

CHAPTER 4 CASTLES

[Pl. 16]
Dundrum Castle, the cylindrical keep, possibly erected by Hugh de Lacy between 1205 and 1210.

CASTLES　　　　　　　　　　　　　　　　　　　　　CHAPTER 4

Dundrum

Tactical considerations therefore played a greater part in the design of the outer walls at Trim than they did in the design of the keep, which represented the ultimate defence of the castle. At the time when the unusual keep at Trim was undergoing construction, a more advanced type was being erected further north in Ulster. This was at Dundrum on the coast of county Down [Pl. 16, Plan 3]. The castle is situated on a hill, 200 feet above the shore, and occupies an excellent strategic position. The site was fortified by John de Courcy soon after his invasion of Ulster in 1177, and over the next two or three decades the initial defences were gradually strengthened, first by a plain curtain wall, then with a stone keep. As with Trim, it is not certain who was responsible for the building work. It may have been John de Courcy before his downfall in 1204, but on architectural grounds it was more probably Hugh de Lacy, who occupied the castle from 1205 to 1210.

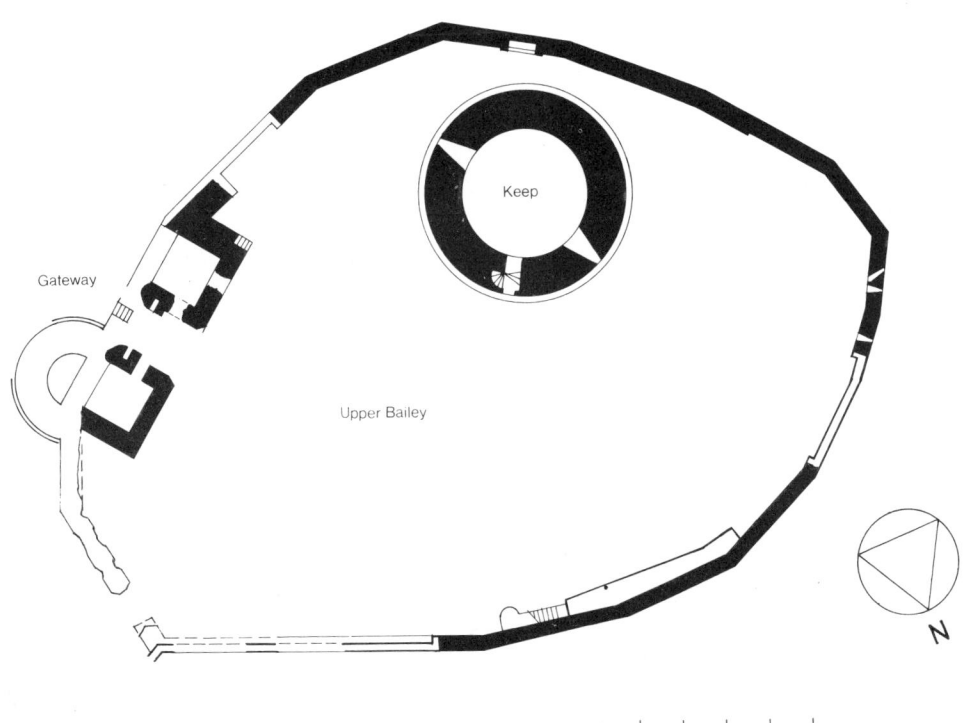

3 Dundrum Castle

CHAPTER 4   CASTLES

The keep at Dundrum is circular in plan, forty-six feet across inside. Above the basement, there were two storeys, reached by a spiral staircase, and at second floor level several narrow chambers were ingeniously fitted into the thickness of the wall. The design is compact and in defensive terms strong. Around 1200 this type of keep became popular, and a number of them can be found in Wales and the Welsh border country—the homeland of many of the Anglo-Normans who invaded Ireland. There is one at Pembroke, for example, erected by William Marshal, lord of Leinster, around 1200, and a slightly earlier one at Longtown in Monmouthshire. Longtown appears to be experimental in character, for there are three vertical bulges on the outside of the cylindrical keep; these contain the staircase, a latrine and the fireplace and its flue, all of which would normally be fitted into the thickness of the wall. It has been tentatively dated to 1187–8 and this date would accord with the experimental nature of the design. As Longtown was constructed by the de Lacy family, this may be the channel through which the idea of the cylindrical keep first reached Ireland.

The cylindrical keep, as well as polygonal variants of it, was adopted at several other thirteenth century castles in Ireland, and a particularly fine one survives at Nenagh in Tipperary. Although strong in defence, however, the circular form was awkward from a residential point of view. It was hard to incorporate into it a hall of reasonable size and proportions, and this explains why the rectangular plan continued to be used, as at Athenry, Maynooth and Greencastle. In these three castles, the keeps—if they can be called that—were designed primarily as spacious halls, rather than impregnable bastions of defence. Thus to some extent a conflict existed between residential and military needs, and this resulted in a re-thinking of castle design during the thirteenth century. The separate keep became increasingly rare, and defence was generally concentrated on a powerful outer wall. This permitted a more flexible arrangement of domestic buildings within the castle, now that they were no longer part of the defensive system.

CASTLES CHAPTER 4

Castleroche

Some of these tendencies are apparent at Castleroche in county Louth [Pl. 17, Plan 4]. This little known castle is among the most spectacular in Ireland, crowning a rocky outcrop in the hills north-west of Dundalk. It was the seat of the de Verdon family, who had first come to Ireland on John's expedition of 1185. The head of the barony was originally at Castletown, about a mile outside Dundalk, but during the thirteenth century it was moved inland to Roche. What induced the de Verdons to make this transfer is not clear, for Castletown was conveniently situated near the sea, whereas Castleroche was more remote and difficult of access. No doubt it was made for some strategic reason, since Castleroche is such an easily defended site, and it may have been intended to protect the expanding settlements in the area. Building probably began soon after 1229, the year in which we are told that Nicholas de Verdon was planning to fortify his lands. Nicholas died two years later, but his daughter Roesia must have continued the work for in 1236 she is described as 'having fortified a castle in her own lands, which none of her predecessors was able to do'.

The layout of the castle was largely dictated by the site, which explains the roughly triangular plan of the curtain walls. On two sides they overlook a cliff, but the third side faced toward a plateau, on which an outer bailey was apparently situated. The main castle is divided from this by a ditch cut through the rock. The only entrance is placed on this side, and it consists of an impressive twin-towered gateway [Pl. 18], with the abutments of the drawbridge still remaining in front. Examination of the masonry suggests that work may have begun on this gateway before the adjoining walls were built up, and for the date 1229–36 it is well in line with the latest developments in England. The twin-towered gateway basically originated in two flanking towers being brought together to guard either side of the entrance, and from the middle of the thirteenth century it became one of the standard features of military architecture. To some extent it took over the role of the keep as the most strongly fortified part of the castle. Such gateways are not uncommon in Ireland, and the castles at Limerick and Ballyloughan have fine examples of them.

Apart from the twin towers of the gate at Castleroche, only one other tower flanked the curtain wall. Presumably it was felt that the

CHAPTER 4 CASTLES

precipitous cliffs below gave adequate protection. Inside the bailey, the main building to survive is a large hall adjoining the curtain wall, through which three windows look out over the valley to the south.

Roche thus provides a good example of a thirteenth century baronial castle in Ireland. The separate keep had now been discarded and defence was based on a powerful gateway with its adjoining curtain walls. A well-proportioned hall was fitted into one corner and this allowed room for a reasonably spacious bailey to cater for the other needs of the castle. At times these included the accommodation of small armies, for in 1332 it was stated that all the free tenants of the barony of Ferrard were accustomed, in the time of Theobald de

4 Castleroche

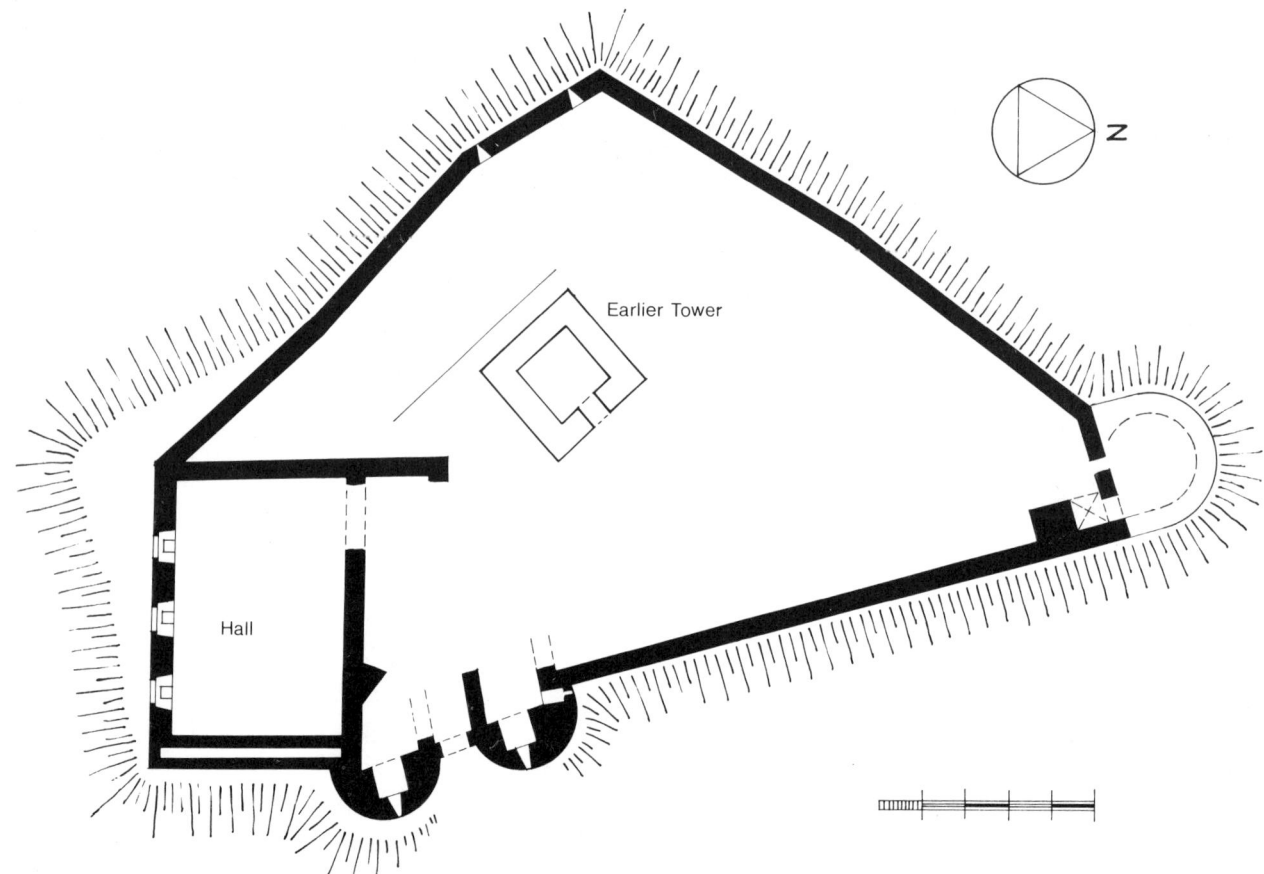

44

CASTLES CHAPTER 4

[Pl. 17]
Castleroche, the stronghold of the de Verdon family in County Louth, built probably between 1229 and 1236.

Verdon (who died in 1316), to do service at Roche when the Irish were at war. However, the history of Castleroche as the centre of a prosperous lordship was shortlived. The manor of Roche evidently suffered badly during the Bruce invasion, for in 1316–17 it was reported that no profit could be received from the lands, and by 1332 the castle itself was lying burnt at the hands of the Irish.

45

CHAPTER 4   CASTLES

[Pl. 18]
Castleroche, the gate-house. The twin-towered gate-house became a standard feature of 13th century military architecture.

CASTLES   CHAPTER 4

Carlow

Although the layout at Castleroche indicates that the isolated keep was no longer considered an essential feature, a small group of castles situated mainly in Leinster retained the idea in a modified form. The square or oblong plan was preserved, but three-quarter round towers were now placed at the angles to strengthen the building at its weakest points. Thus the advantages of the square and circular keeps were combined while their faults were avoided. No vulnerable corners faced the enemy and there was plenty of space to include halls and chambers of fine proportion. The best preserved keeps of this type are found at Lea, in county Laois, at Ferns and Carlow. There are no parallels for the design in England at this period, though the scheme was employed there in the later middle ages. A fine example survives at Nunney in Somerset (c. 1373). Most of the Irish keeps of this type date from the thirteenth century, but as yet no adequate study has been made of them. Since the plans are similar and the castles geographically close, they may all derive from a common prototype somewhere in Leinster. Whether this was a castle now destroyed or one of the survivors is hard to say. None of the buildings can be precisely dated, nor is there any apparent dynastic link between them which might explain the common design.

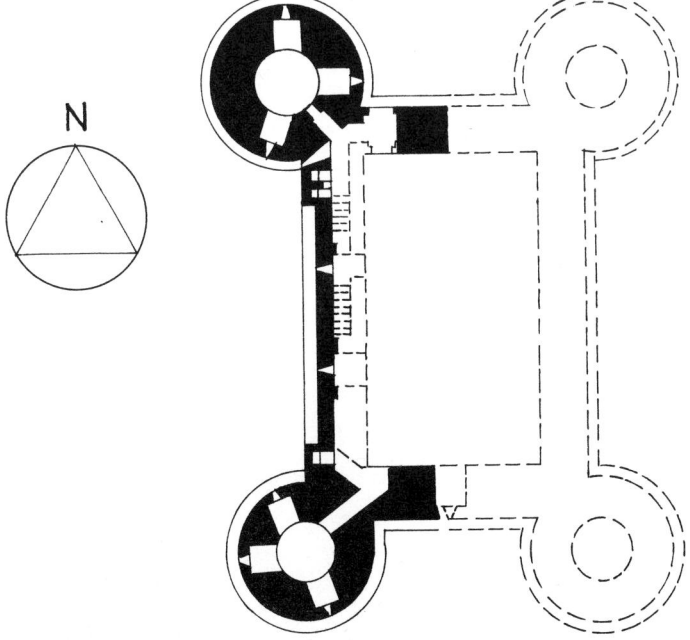

5   Carlow Castle

CHAPTER 4　　　　　　CASTLES

Carlow may well be the earliest in the group. Only one wall and two of its towers remain [Pl. 19, Plan 5]; the rest was blown up in 1814 in an attempt to make room for a lunatic asylum. Early engravings and drawings show the castle in a more complete condition [Pl. 20], and when used in conjunction with the existing remains, one can get a reasonable impression of its medieval appearance. None of the surviving masonry offers any precise clues about dating, but the

[Pl. 19]
Carlow Castle, ruins of the keep.

CASTLES CHAPTER 4

construction of the castle has been ascribed either to William Marshal when he was in Leinster from 1207 to 1213, or to his son who succeeded to the lordship in 1219. A castle already existed before this but presumably it was a motte and bailey fortification. The first quarter of the thirteenth century is certainly a likely time for such a castle to be rebuilt in stone. The engravings show small round-headed windows which would accord with this early date, although the artist's interpretation may not be wholly reliable. Finally there is one piece of evidence which suggests the castle was already quite old by 1307.

[Pl. 20] Carlow Castle, the Beranger drawing of the late eighteenth century shows the keep nearly intact.

CHAPTER 4 CASTLES

This is the report of an inquisition into the lands of Roger Bigod and it contains a brief mention of the establishment at Carlow. After stressing that the castle is 'badly roofed', it continues: 'opposite the castle is a hall in which pleas of the county and of the assize are held; in the castle and hall there are many defects, as well in the roof as in the walls, so that they can be extended at no price; no one would rent them. They greatly want roofing and good keeping'. Too much should not be read into this report of deterioration, for even new buildings in the middle ages were as quick to decay as their modern counterparts. But taken with the other evidence it suggests that the first half of the century is the most likely period for construction. It would be pleasant to ascribe the novel design of the keep to William Marshal's patronage, but although an attractive suggestion, it is impossible to prove.

Dublin

The Carlow design seems to have been restricted to private lords, for there is no evidence that any of the royal castles took this form. Indeed keeps are rare in works of the Crown, although the rectangular one at Randown is an obvious exception. In most cases the plan was based on a powerful curtain wall as at Dublin and Roscommon, two castles about which a great deal of documentary evidence survives. Dublin was the most important of the Irish castles and it is therefore a great pity that eighteenth century reconstruction has largely obliterated the medieval buildings. A plan of the layout was made about 1685, before rebuilding started, and it shows an almost rectangular bailey surrounded by a curtain wall with round towers at the four angles. The remnants of two of these survive in the towers now known as the Record Tower and the Birmingham Tower. Since Dublin was the centre of the royal government, there were a number of administrative buildings, not to mention Henry III's splendid hall of 1243–5. There is, however, no evidence of a free-standing keep.

The earliest reference to a castle in Dublin is in the year 1172, so it appears the Anglo-Normans set about constructing it as soon as they had taken the city. Like almost all their early fortifications it seems to have been a motte and bailey castle, intended primarily for defensive purposes. But in 1204 the King decided that a more substantial building should be erected, since there was no suitable place in which

CASTLES CHAPTER 4

to deposit the royal treasure. He thus ordered the justiciar of Ireland 'to cause a castle to be constructed in Dublin for the uses of justice in the city, and if need be for the city's defence, with good dikes and strong walls'. The mention of the royal treasure and the needs of justice immediately reveal the vital administrative rôle of the castle. There are continual references to building operations up until 1229. In this year both carpenters and masons were paid 'for making towers' and there was also a payment of £8 12s 2½d for six loads of lead, its transport to the castle, and its conversion into gutters for the towers, suggesting that one or two of them were nearing completion. At various later periods further extensive work took place. Between 1279 and 1284, when Thomas Burel was keeper of the works, over five hundred pounds were spent, though there is no evidence to show exactly what was under construction.

From the various fragmentary records, it is possible to build up a reasonable picture of the thirteenth century castle. About 1224 an inventory of stores was made, which mentions many of the rooms. After listing the stocks of arms, it refers to 'one great chest in the chamber, another in the chamber beyond the sheriff's chamber, and another in the alms hall'. The precise position of these four rooms is not known. Then it describes the contents of the workshop where there was 'a great chain to guard the prisoners, and another for the bridge'—presumably part of the lifting gear for the drawbridge. The next rooms to be mentioned are the kitchen and butlery, which apart from one hundred dishes seemed to be grossly inadequately stocked—only one cauldron, two platters, five cups and five pitchers!

Eleven years later in 1235 a new kitchen had to be built after part of the castle collapsed and in the same year there were payments for building an engine house and a house for the delivery of meat. In 1240 there is a reference to 'the King's chamber' and then three years later the great new hall was begun. At the same time attention was being paid to the castle chapel, for in 1242 the King sent an order requiring 'the glass windows' to be made. As well as all these chambers and apartments, the Exchequer was evidently housed in the castle or at least adjoined it.

The equipment and buildings of the castle inevitably needed constant

CHAPTER 4   CASTLES

maintenance and there are many references to repairs. In 1275–6, for example, twenty shillings was needed to repair the drawbridge, and at the same time substantial sums had to be spent on 'the tower of the gate' which had been burned by Hubert de Burgh and his accomplices when they had been confined in prison there.

The rich supply of information about the thirteenth century work makes it all the more disappointing that so little survives of the original medieval buildings. The records clearly show that an elaborate complex once existed within the curtain walls. The need to incorporate a diverse range of buildings explains why the castle was planned with a large rectangular bailey, and why defence was concentrated on the outer walls and towers rather than on a single stronghold inside.

Roscommon

During the 1270s and 1280s the royal government spent large sums of money on castle-building. The new castle of Mackynegan (Newcastle, county Wicklow) was started at this time, part of an attempt to control the Irish in the Wicklow mountains. But more lavish expenditure was undertaken in Connaught. One completely new castle was begun at Roscommon, and two older ones at Randown and Athlone greatly strengthened. Roscommon is the most interesting of the three, since it provides a good indication of the latest ideas on military design in government circles.

The castle was built on land belonging to the priory of St. Coman at Roscommon, apparently without permission, and from the priory's complaints we learn how the site was chosen. In 1269 Robert de Ufford, justiciar of Ireland, perambulated the whole cantred of Roscommon together with the greater men of the council and found no place 'so suitable, firm and worthy as in the tenement of our church of Roscommon near the lake vulgarly called Lochnanen' where he proceeded to build a castle without their consent or that of the bishop. The lake has now vanished and with it part of the natural defence of the castle. Perhaps one should also add that the canons received land in compensation for what they had lost—though not until 1281.

Building operations after 1269 were badly interrupted by Irish attacks.

CASTLES CHAPTER 4

In 1272 the castle was demolished by Hugh O Connor and five years later he returned and repeated the operation. Not despairing, in 1280 the government embarked on a massive campaign of building, no doubt in an effort to make the fortifications quite impregnable. To what extent the original plan was revised at this stage is impossible to determine, but it seems that the design was considerably enlarged. The square gate-tower which faces west may be a survival from the earlier work, for it is not aligned to the walls on either side [Pl. 21].

In 1280 Robert de Ufford accounted for £3,200 2s 5d spent on the

[Pl. 21] Roscommon Castle, from the west (1280–5). The postern gate may be a survival from the earlier castle.

CHAPTER 4   CASTLES

three castles defending Connaught, and much of this must have gone on work at Roscommon. For the next five years there are many further references to expenditure on the castle, where operations were evidently controlled by Gregory de Coquile, the keeper of the works. However, other royal officials were also involved, in particular William de Spineto, later Sheriff of Uriel (Louth). In 1284 he was 'engaged at making a wall around the castle', but his exact rôle is not clear. He was basically a government administrator, and therefore likely to be involved more in financial matters than in the supervision of the masons.

The source of the stone used is not yet known, but many of the subsidiary materials—nails, iron and pitch for example—were brought out from Dublin, a difficult overland journey. The records include several payments for the hire of carts to carry provisions and other stores. Building seems to have slowed down after 1285, which may indicate that the castle was nearing completion, but for the next two decades or more there was still work to be done. It was at Roscommon that William de Prene, the king's carpenter, went about many of his nefarious activities in the years before 1292. Then in 1304 Richard of Exeter, keeper of the castle, was engaged on repairs and minor works, and his account gives a lot of information about the castle. The three drawbridges needed attention, so too did the portcullises of the two gates. Then there is a reference to 'the two outer bridges', suggesting there may have been more than one ditch encircling the castle. The steps at the entry to the hall also needed repair—the first reference to the existence of a hall. Forty shillings were also spent on 'the repair of the well of the castle and strengthening it with stone of the thickness of three feet, so that it may remain of the breadth of five feet, and a depth of thirty-two feet'. The money also included the price of a wooden cover.

As Gregory de Coquile is cited as 'keeper of the works' between 1280 and 1285, the design of Roscommon was presumably his responsibility. It consists of a huge courtyard measuring 162 feet by 130 feet contained within the curtain wall [Pl. 22, Plan 6]. A round tower is placed at each angle, and on the east side away from the former lake are the remains of a twin-towered gateway. The rectangular curtain was surrounded by an equally symmetrical moat, the line of which

CASTLES CHAPTER 4

can be traced in the neighbouring fields—this may in fact be the outer of two moats, though no trace of the inner one survives. Gregory de Coquile—or whoever designed the castle—was clearly familiar with the latest views in royal circles, for the plan bears a close relationship with some of the work carried out in North Wales under Edward I. The lay-out of the main walls at Harlech, started three years after Roscommon in 1283, is fundamentally the same, though the Welsh castle has a second curtain wall enclosing an outer bailey. One wonders whether Gregory de Coquile received his training in Wales,

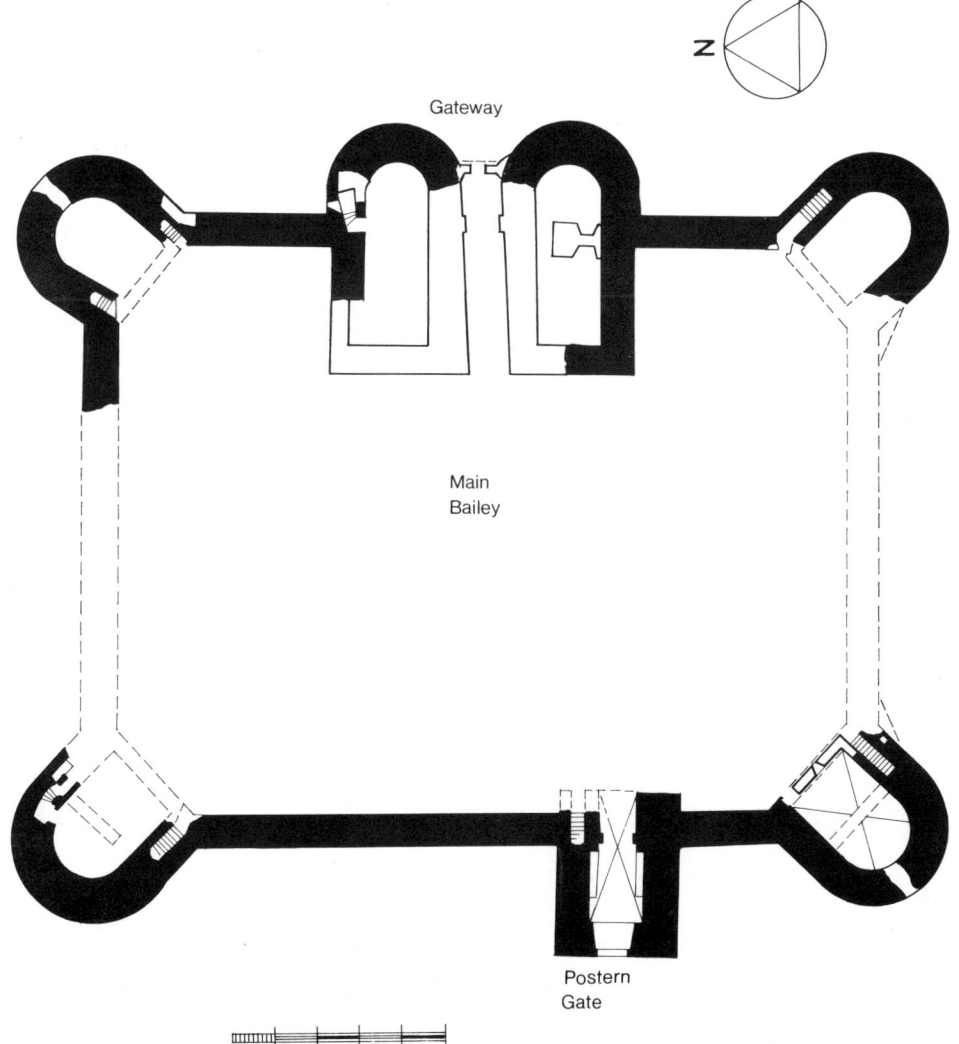

6 Roscommon Castle

CHAPTER 4   CASTLES

but there is apparently no reference to him in the English records.

The construction of the royal castle of Roscommon represents a climax in Anglo-Norman military architecture in Ireland. It set the pattern for several others, of which Ballymote in County Sligo is the best preserved. Only ten miles from Roscommon, at Ballintubber, there is an Irish version of the scheme, though with polygonal towers

[Pl. 22] Roscommon Castle, the layout of the castle is clear from the aerial view.

in place of circular ones. The design of Roscommon reflected the latest ideas current in England and Wales and reminds us that the Irish castles of this period were not as outdated as is commonly imagined. Despite its battering by the Cromwellians in 1652, it remains an impressive fortress, a monument to the Anglo-Normans' determination to establish firm control over the Irish of Connaught.

CHAPTER 5   CATHEDRALS

For a small country, Ireland is divided into an astonishing number of dioceses—one of the legacies of Celtic organisation. During the middle ages they were even more numerous, so inevitably each diocese was small, and the money available for building limited. Thus the traveller should not be surprised by the tiny scale of many an Irish cathedral, often situated in towns and villages which are remarkable only for their ecclesiastical importance. Indeed the rôle of a cathedral in Ireland was in some ways more akin to that of an English parish church.

During the late twelfth and thirteenth centuries a considerable proportion of these cathedrals were reconstructed, most of them in the early Gothic style brought over from England by the Anglo-Normans. Not surprisingly, therefore, the artistic connections between the two countries were close. The various designs employed at Waterford, Kilkenny and St. Patrick's, Dublin must have been drawn up by masons familiar with contemporary architecture in England and, in the case of Christ Church, Dublin, one can be sure that English masons were recruited to execute the work.

Christ Church Cathedral
Christ Church is perhaps the finest of the early medieval cathedrals. The building has been viciously treated by the nineteenth century restorers and its gloomy interior scarcely inspires enthusiasm. But one should not be dismayed by the initial impression. A search into the shadows reveals carving of rare quality, and enough ancient masonry survives to allow us to picture the church in its original splendour.

A cathedral existed in Dublin before the arrival of the Anglo-Normans but clearly the invaders regarded it with disdain and set about the task of reconstruction. This probably began soon after 1181 when John Comyn was appointed archbishop. The surviving work falls into two phases. Building began in a late Romanesque style with the choir and transepts and then there followed an interruption of perhaps a decade. About 1213 work was resumed on the nave, this time in an early Gothic style. The cathedral was finished around 1240 but it has been drastically altered since then. A vast new choir was added in the fourteenth century which was demolished 100 years ago when the

CHAPTER 5 — CATHEDRALS

architect in charge, G. E. Street, tried to restore it to what he supposed had been the original Romanesque appearance. He also rebuilt the south elevation of the nave. Consequently one has to look hard to distinguish medieval work from Victorian restoration. The transepts still retain much that is Romanesque and most of the north elevation of the nave is genuine early Gothic. Elsewhere only fragments of medieval masonry survive.

The crypt however has remained untouched and, by studying its plan, the original layout of the church can be surmised [Plan 7]. The most curious feature is the termination of the choir in a sort of polygonal apse. An ambulatory runs round it and three chapels lead off to the east. This ingenious if slightly clumsy arrangement is most unusual. It may have been suggested by John Comyn, the archbishop, who came from an area where the only parallels for it can be found. Before coming to Dublin he is said to have been a monk at Evesham, and although the church there has been destroyed, both the neighbouring abbeys of Tewkesbury and Pershore and the cathedral of Gloucester had a similar layout. All three churches must have been familiar to Comyn.

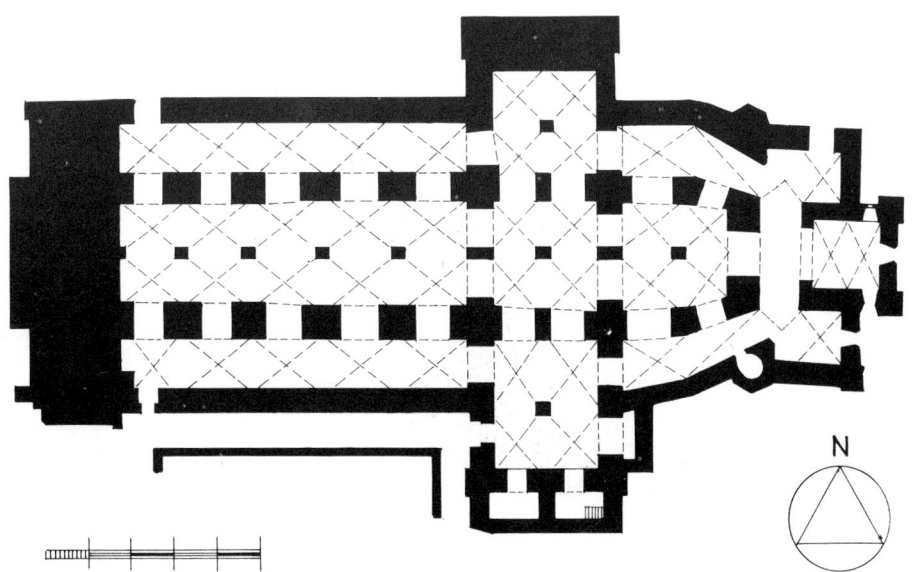

7 Christ Church Cathedral, crypt

CHAPTER 5   CATHEDRALS

The resulting plan of Christ Church is more complicated than that found anywhere else in Ireland. The only other church with an ambulatory is the nearby cathedral of St. Patrick, where the plan also derives from an English model. But for the most part, Irish cathedrals display no concern for elaborate architecture at the east end. Even aisles were almost unknown, so that the usual choir is little more than a long rectangular chamber. Against this background, the twelfth century plan of Christ Church appears as one of the more enterprising schemes in the country.

Like G. E. Street we can only guess what the elevation of the choir looked like, though the surviving transepts provide some impression. The walls here are extremely thick, for this was essential to withstand the thrusts of the stone vault above. At both clerestory and triforium level a passage runs within the thickness of the wall, and the various arches opening into it are decorated with elaborate chevron, the zig-zag ornament so favoured in the twelfth century.

The sculpture of Christ Church
Both choir and transepts received a series of richly carved capitals, some still *in situ,* a few preserved in the crypt. The style of this sculpture suggests that the mason responsible came from Somerset for there are many similarities with contemporary work at Wells Cathedral and Glastonbury Abbey. Again the career of John Comyn may explain the connection. For two years from 1180–1 he was abbot of Glastonbury, and he could have been instrumental in bringing one of the local masons over to Dublin when he was appointed archbishop in 1181.

Perhaps the most attractive capital is one in the north transept depicting two human busts surrounded by winged dragons [Pl. 23]. The skill and experience of the sculptor is clearly evident, for not only is the composition well designed, but the cutting is deep and confident. The two projecting faces, which neatly stress the angle of the capital, are not unlike one on a corbel in the south transept at Wells.

CATHEDRALS CHAPTER 5

[Pl. 23]
Christ Church Cathedral, Dublin, capital in the north transept (c. 1190).

Nearby is a capital with several full length figures attired in flowing robes [Pl. 24]. The subject of the carving is hard to interpret, but it may have a religious meaning, since a strange demon-like character is depicted at one corner. The carving of the robes with their long vertical folds is similar to the technique used for some of the figures on the north doorway of the Lady Chapel at Glastonbury. This was built soon after 1184 and the sculpture at Christ Church must be of a similar date.

CHAPTER 5 CATHEDRALS

[Pl. 24]
Christ Church Cathedral, Dublin, capital in the north transept (c. 1190).

Apart from this capital, the other carving in the cathedral has little semblance of religious meaning. Animals, human figures and foliage designs form the basic repertoire. In the choir there are a few capitals which survived the various reconstructions, and one of these depicts fruit-gatherers, a subject also found at Wells.

The quality of this Christ Church sculpture has for long been un-recognised, and two of the most exciting fragments have lain un-noticed in the darkness of the crypt. One of these stones apparently

CHAPTER 5 — CATHEDRALS

[Pl. 25]
Christ Church Cathedral, Dublin,
carved fragment in the crypt
(c. 1190).

formed the top of an arch [Pl. 25], where a head was carved gripping one of the mouldings in its mouth—a unique and imaginative idea. The other was a capital carved in the form of a monster head, with bulging eyes and rounded cheeks [Pl. 26]. Again the confidence of the sculptor is apparent. Such monster-head capitals occur quite frequently in the western counties of England—they appear at

CHAPTER 5 CATHEDRALS

Christ Church Cathedral, Dublin, capital preserved in the crypt (c. 1190).

Malmesbury Abbey, for example—and it provides further proof that this was the area from which the Christ Church masons were recruited. Their approach to stone carving was a contrast to that of the native Irish craftsmen, for they were prepared to cut more vigorously into the stone and the designs they used came from a different tradition. Sculpture like that on the Nun's Church at Clonmacnoise [Pl. 2], erected only twenty years or so before, seems very flat in comparison.

CATHEDRALS

CHAPTER 5

[Pl. 27]
Christ Church
Cathedral, Dublin,
north elevation of the nave
(c. 1213–34).

CHAPTER 5   CATHEDRALS

[Pl. 28]
Pershore Abbey, choir, consecrated 1239.

Christ Church, the design of the nave

The first building campaign must have come to a halt about 1200. When work was resumed a decade later, a new master mason was in charge, the man whom it is easiest to call the Christ Church master. As already shown he came from Worcestershire, where he had previously worked at Droitwich and Overbury. His task at Christ Church was altogether on a grander scale, but the design he produced is elegant and imposing, and shows that he had mastered the latest architectural developments in the west of England.

To judge his design one must look at the north elevation of the nave, which has survived relatively unscathed [Pl. 27]. He divided it into two roughly equal parts with a horizontal string course separating the main arcades below from the triforium and clerestory above. To lead the eye upwards over this division he placed a shaft running from the base of the pier to the springing of the vault. In this way a pleasing balance between horizontal and vertical was obtained. The main piers are relatively low and massive in proportion, and this accords with the general taste in the west of England at the time. They are embellished with a series of attached shafts, banded half way, and the arches they support are carved with elaborate mouldings on the underside. The deep shadows which result add to the overall linear pattern of the architecture.

So far none of this was particularly unusual. But in the upper parts of the design, the Christ Church master revealed his imagination and quality as an architect. Here he integrated the triforium and clerestory, normally two separate stages, into one coherent design. Slender shafts of black marble rise from the level of the string course and link the three arches of the triforium with the three windows of the clerestory above. Again a comfortable balance between horizontal and vertical was achieved.

Similar experiments at integration had occurred in England and Wales, though none of the solutions was as effective as Christ Church. The most relevant is the choir of Pershore Abbey, consecrated in 1239 [Pl. 28]. Pershore is situated in Worcestershire not far from the English churches where the Christ Church master had previously worked. The solution there is more extreme, for the arches of the triforium were completely removed; there is nothing to break the

[Pl. 29]
Christ Church Cathedral, Dublin, capital in the nave (c. 1220).

vertical emphasis and the subtle balance of Christ Church is lost. But the designs of both churches seem to reflect a similar idea, apparently current in the Worcestershire workshops of the early thirteenth century.

The Christ Church master

The evidence at Overbury and Droitwich suggested that the Christ Church master also controlled the sculptural details of his buildings. Much of his carving in Dublin has been destroyed but some remains amidst the harsh Victorian copies. Thick bunches of foliage form the basic ornament, the 'stiff leaf' which became the convention at this time [Pl. 10]. Occasionally human heads—some with crowns—peer out between the leaves, their expressions placid, apart from one

CHAPTER 5   CATHEDRALS

shrouded face which scowls in pain [Pl. 29]. The carving of the heads is not exactly beautiful, the mouths in particular are narrow and mean, but the technique is exceedingly competent. This combination of heads and foliage occurs in several churches in the west of Britain, and the ultimate source of the formula appears to be the sculpture of Wells Cathedral.

The Christ Church master was undoubtedly one of the foremost craftsmen to work in Ireland during the thirteenth century. As a sculptor his style may have lacked sensitivity, but as an architect he was outstanding. He was employed in Ireland for perhaps twenty years. He disappeared from the scene about 1234, the year in which the prior and canons of Christ Church were given permission to extend their church at the west. This must refer to the last bay of the nave which was clearly an afterthought since there is no corresponding bay in the crypt below. The work was carried out by a new master mason. The capitals are carved in a different form and the mouldings of the arch have a different profile. The main elements in the design, however, were preserved to ensure continuity. The style of the Christ Church master remained unique in Ireland, and it does not appear to have exercised any substantial influence. Only the west window at Boyle Abbey [Pl. 51] shows traces of his manner for it has the banded shafts and other details which occur on the windows in Dublin. It may indeed be his final work.

St. Patrick's Cathedral
The one design which can compare with the nave of Christ Church is to be found a few hundred yards away in the cathedral of St. Patrick. The approach is very different, perhaps deliberately so. The interior is more spacious and there is a greater feeling of harmony, for unlike Christ Church there were no prolonged halts in building operations to cause a fundamental break in style. St. Patrick's was probably begun about 1225, the year in which preachers were sent out into the country to beg alms for the building. The cathedral was consecrated in 1254, though this does not necessarily imply it was finished by then. Its history has been as disastrous as its neighbour's, suffering partial ruin and undergoing the inevitable Victorian restora-

CATHEDRALS CHAPTER 5

tion. But in the choir and south transept much remains that is authentically medieval.

The plan of the choir is usually compared with Salisbury, for they both have a large aisled chapel opening off a square ambulatory. At St. Patrick's, however, the chapel seems to be an addition of c. 1270 for some of its details differ from the adjoining parts of the choir. So the original plans would not have looked similar. Nor is the elevation much like Salisbury, though the sources of its design are to be found in English churches of the west country. The abundance of stiff leaf carving and the rich mouldings of the arches are significant in this respect.

The design of the upper parts of the elevation is more orthodox than Christ Church, for the triforium and clerestory stages are clearly separate from each other [Pl. 30]. There are twin arches in the triforium, but the clerestory windows above are divided into three, a tall central one and a lower one either side. The basic source for this arrangement may be the type of design employed in the choir of Worcester Cathedral, finished in 1231. Many of the mouldings in St. Patrick's are continued unbroken round the arch with no intervening capital, and often such mouldings are used in conjunction with the more normal form of column and arch. The technique helps to enliven the design and prevent monotony, and it was a conspicuous feature of English west country architecture in the late twelfth and early thirteenth century.

Unfortunately the design used in the choir was simplified as work proceeded westwards. Perhaps resources were insufficient to pay for such elaboration and the authorities were no doubt impatient to complete the church. In the transept the piers were simplified and the number of arch mouldings reduced. In the nave the architecture became even more austere. Had the choir design been repeated throughout the building, St. Patrick's would have become one of the supreme essays in the 'early English' style. Even so, it proved more influential than Christ Church. The simplified form of pier and arch used in the transept provided a convenient prototype, and similar ones were designed at Mellifont, Kildare and the cathedral of Kilkenny.

[Pl. 30]
St. Patrick's Cathedral, Dublin, north elevation of the choir (c. 1230). The linear qualities of the 'early English' style are clearly evident in the photograph.

But for the most part the Dublin churches were too lavish to be much help to the smaller Irish cathedrals. With their low stocky piers, their profusion of mouldings, and their decorative use of black marble shafts, they fit neatly into the pattern of early English Gothic. They are the only two thirteenth century churches in Ireland designed on a truly grand scale. They both have ambulatories in the choir, they both have three stage elevations and they were both covered by stone rib vaults. No such combination of features exists elsewhere. The main vaults in both cathedrals have since been replaced by modern copies, but in the aisles of St. Patrick some of the medieval ribs survive.

Newtown Trim Cathedral
The construction of vaults presented the medieval mason with his most formidable task, and it is disappointing to find that so few were built in Ireland and that even fewer survive. The Cistercians normally constructed them in the chancels of their abbeys, and one other cathedral certainly vaulted was that at Newtown Trim. This was founded in 1206 on the banks of the river Boyne about a mile downstream from Trim Castle. The huge church is now ruined and parts of it have vanished completely, but built into the walls of the former nave one or two of the springers for the vault remain.

Waterford Cathedral
The demolition in 1773 of the old cathedral in Waterford removed one of the most fascinating pieces of medieval architecture in Ireland. The church was not as large or as splendid as those in Dublin, but an old picture shows that the interior elevation was modelled on the design of Glastonbury. Here a huge arch encloses both main arcade and triforium. It reminds us once again that the two Somerset workshops of Wells and Glastonbury exercised a vital influence on the medieval architecture and sculpture of Ireland.

St. Canice's, Kilkenny
Destruction, decay and over-zealous restoration have left us with few ecclesiastical interiors that retain any of their original atmosphere.

[Pl. 31] St. Canice's Cathedral, Kilkenny, the choir (first half of the 13th century).

One of the exceptions is St. Canice's at Kilkenny [Pl. 31, 32]. Here there is a wonderful sense of light and space, the architecture simple and unadorned, the building not too cluttered by later accretions.

Although large, it was not a particularly ambitious church. There were no vaults, the plan is straightforward, and the elevations are free

[Pl. 32] St. Canice's Cathedral, Kilkenny, the nave (mid-13th century).

from complexity. It was started by Hugh de Rous the first Anglo-Norman bishop of Ossory (1202–18). As was so often the case, it appears the Anglo-Norman had a more splendid conception of the rôle of a cathedral than did his Irish predecessors. The existing Romanesque building no doubt seemed inadequate, and he embarked on a church which to him more befitted the rank of cathedral. By 1256 the work was nearing completion, and it was probably finished within the next few years. A building campaign lasting from c.1210

CHAPTER 5　　　CATHEDRALS

to c.1260 accords with the style of the architecture. The design of the three east windows in the choir [Pl. 31], for instance, is similar to those in the Cistercian abbey of Graiguenamanagh founded c.1207, and it has been suggested that the same group of masons was responsible for work in both churches.

The design of the choir at Kilkenny is more typical of Gothic in Ireland than either of the two Dublin cathedrals—a straightforward rectangular plan, a wooden roof and tall lancet windows. With variations of detail this is the standard form all over the country in the thirteenth century [Plan 8]. Since he had no worries about supporting a stone vault, the master mason was free to open large windows in the wall below. As a result light floods into the sanctuary from a series of windows, grouped in threes. Inside they are decorated with detached shafts of black marble, and the trefoiled rear arches above are furnished with dog-tooth ornament, the stock motif of the 'early English' style.

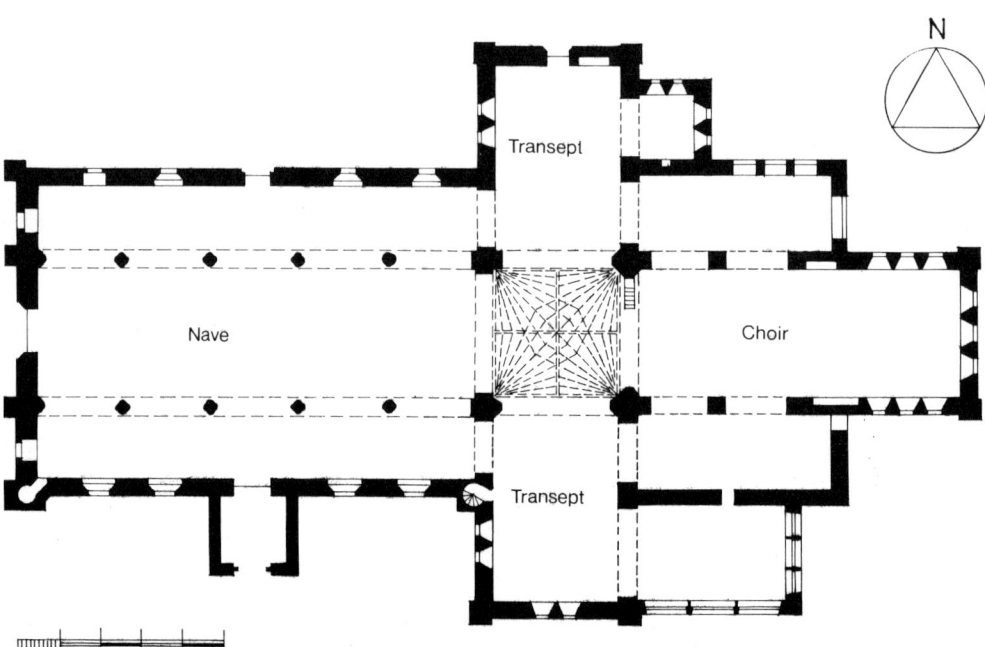

8　Kilkenny Cathedral

CHAPTER 5   CATHEDRALS

The Gowran master

In the nave there is a change in design which suggests that by now different masons were employed [Pl. 32]. The master mason in charge can be traced elsewhere in the locality. The ruined church at Gowran, eight miles away to the east, was almost certainly his responsibility and since we do not know his name, it is convenient to refer to him as the Gowran master. The characteristics of his style also appear at Thomastown, though only one arcade of this building remains.

None of the three churches was vaulted and this permitted greater freedom in their design. The piers were placed wide apart, giving an open spacious feeling to the interior which would have been impossible if a stone vault had to be supported above. The broad arches rest on rather squat piers which are given a distinctive quatrefoil shape. Both bases and capitals are furnished with robust horizontal mouldings. At Kilkenny and Gowran the quatrefoil shape is repeated in the form of the clerestory windows, a subtle device which adds to the harmony of the design. Among other characteristics of the Gowran master is a preference for certain types of window. Thus some of those at Gowran and Thomastown consist simply of two paired lancets, and a more elaborate version with a quatrefoil added in the spandrel is also found at Gowran as well as in St. Canice's at Kilkenny.

As a sculptor the Gowran master was perhaps the most gifted craftsman to work in Ireland during the thirteenth century. Unfortunately his carving was largely restricted to capitals and corbels, though it is possible that a tomb effigy preserved at New Ross is an example of his work. Elsewhere, however, foliage and heads form the basic repertoire. The faces which he carved were more varied and human than those of the Christ Church master. Often they seem to smile, and their broad mouths and thick lips give them an almost sensuous quality. The decoration of a tomb recess in the north transept at Kilkenny illustrates some of these characteristics [Pl. 33]. On the capitals tiny faces gaze out between rosettes; just above, the label stop takes the form of a female head, staring determinedly forward. It is worth noticing the shape of the eyes and the detailed cutting of the eyelids, for these are conspicuous features of the sculptor's style.

CHAPTER 5 CATHEDRALS

[Pl. 33]
St. Canice's Cathedral, Kilkenny, tomb recess in the north transept (c. 1260).

More of his work is found on the south porch but this is badly weathered. So too is the west doorway, the finest of the early Gothic doorways to survive in Ireland [Pl. 34]. The main arch is subdivided and each of these smaller openings is decorated with foliage cusps. In the spandrel above is a quatrefoil frame, now bare although originally it must have contained a carving of the Virgin and Child. Here the full potential of the Gowran master might once have been evident. Either side are smaller quatrefoils containing angels who kneel in adoration, and the blank spaces around are filled by circular

CATHEDRALS
CHAPTER 5

[Pl. 34]
St. Canice's Cathedral, Kilkenny,
the west door (c. 1260).

bosses, intricately carved with foliage. The general design seems to be an elaboration of the west doorway at Wells Cathedral carved c. 1245 [Pl. 35]. There one finds similar twin arches, a quatrefoil above, and adoring angels either side. Intricate foliage bosses, though not on the doorway, occur repeatedly in the cathedral. The Kilkenny door must be about fifteen years later to judge from the advance in

[Pl. 35]
Wells Cathedral, the west door (c. 1245).

[Pl. 36]
Gowran, detail from a tomb recess (c. 1260).

style, and a date c. 1260 fits what the documentary sources tell us about the progress of building.

At about the same time the Gowran master must also have been working at Gowran itself, which is the best place to examine his style. Here there are many fine heads decorating the various windows and tomb recesses [Pl. 36]. The majority are badly weathered, but high on the west window almost out of sight are four magnificent ones, remarkably well preserved.

The close relationship between architectural and sculptural details at Gowran seems to confirm that both aspects were the responsibility of a single directing hand. A clear illustration of this is the beautiful

[Pl. 37]
Gowran, east window in south aisle of the nave (c. 1260).

window at the east end of the south aisle [Pl. 37]. It is divided into two parts by the thickness of the wall, forming an inner and an outer frame. The inner frame is subdivided and each of the subsidiary arches has a trefoil head, while above in the spandrel is a quatrefoil. There are many foliage cusps, as in the west doorway at Kilkenny, and the subsidiary arches are embellished with dog tooth. On the right side, the hood mould terminates in one of those elegant heads so typical of the Gowran master's work.

The three churches at Gowran, Thomastown and Kilkenny form one of the most attractive groups in Ireland, and it is a tragedy that two of them have been so devastated in the course of time. But at least St. Canice's survives to remind us of the Gowran master's architectural design, and from the many battered remnants of his carving, there is enough to show his skill and sensitivity as a sculptor.

CATHEDRALS CHAPTER 5

St. Mary's, New Ross

Although serving only a parish, the large church of St. Mary's, New Ross was designed on a scale as grand as most Irish cathedrals [Pl. 38, Plan 9]. New Ross itself was a thriving town in the thirteenth century. Founded soon after 1192 under the auspices of William Marshal, lord of Leinster from 1189 to 1219, it had become by 1275 one of the most flourishing ports in Ireland. It was natural that the local church should in some way reflect this mercantile splendour. The discovery within the church of a memorial stone to William Marshal's wife Isabella, suggests that he himself may have been the founder. The style of the architecture confirms that it was started during his lifetime.

As so often in Ireland, only fragments of the building have survived. The nave has been totally destroyed and in its place stands a nineteenth century church. Beyond lie the impressive remains of the old

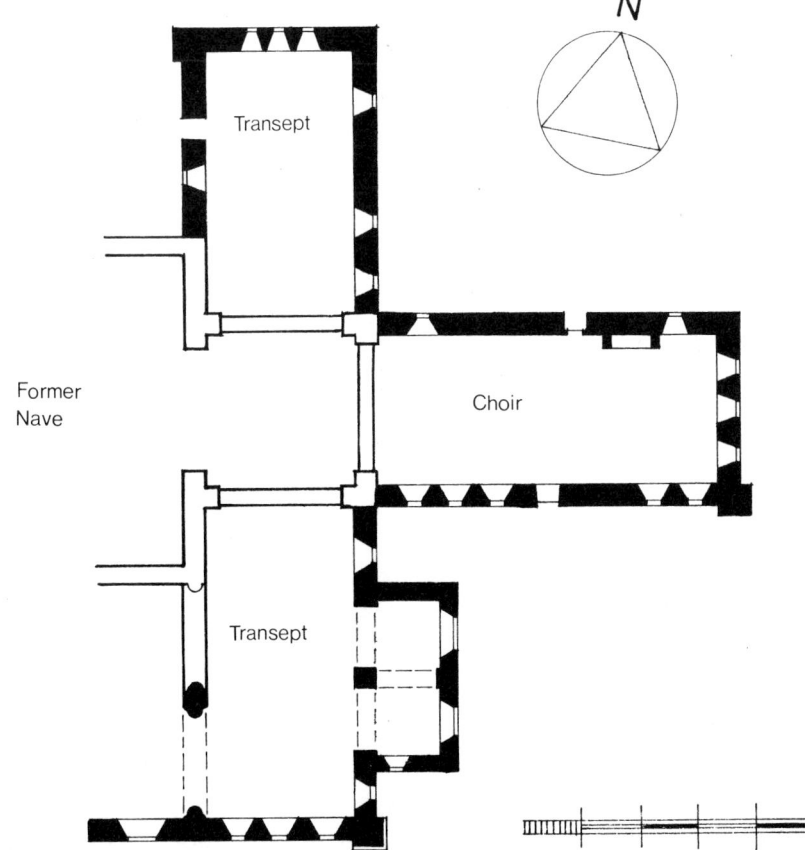

9 New Ross, St. Mary's

St. Mary's, New Ross, choir (first quarter 13th century).

[Pl. 39]
St. Mary's, New Ross, capital from piscina in the choir.

choir and transepts. The early Gothic choir, with its tall lancet windows and delicate mouldings, is a design of simple beauty, but the quality of the ornament seems crude compared to the work that the Gowran master was to produce several decades later. Built into the south wall of the choir is a piscina, consisting of a trefoiled arch resting on angle shafts. The carving on the capitals is typical of the decoration throughout the church, vigorous and striking, if slightly bizarre [Pl. 39].

CHAPTER 5 CATHEDRALS

Cashel Cathedral

Similar carving is to be found on the early parts of Cashel Cathedral, and it is not impossible that one of the New Ross masons afterwards moved on there. Some of the capitals are especially alike, as well as the heads which form the label stops. The cathedral, dramatically situated on the famous rock, was squeezed tightly between the old Round Tower and Cormac's Chapel [Pl. 40, Plan 10]. It replaced an earlier building begun about sixty years before, and the desire to rebuild provides a striking indication of the spread of grander ideas about architecture. Reconstruction was not, however, undertaken by some lordly Anglo-Norman ecclesiastic, for Irishmen held the see throughout the period and so Cashel provides an example of native patronage. Archbishop Marianus O'Brien (1224–38) is usually credited with the start of work.

In its general design as well as its details, the choir is similar to New Ross—exceptionally long, with no aisles and lit by a series of tall lancet windows. However, in one respect Cashel is unique. Above the lancets are tiny windows fitted into the spandrels [Pl. 41]. Outside

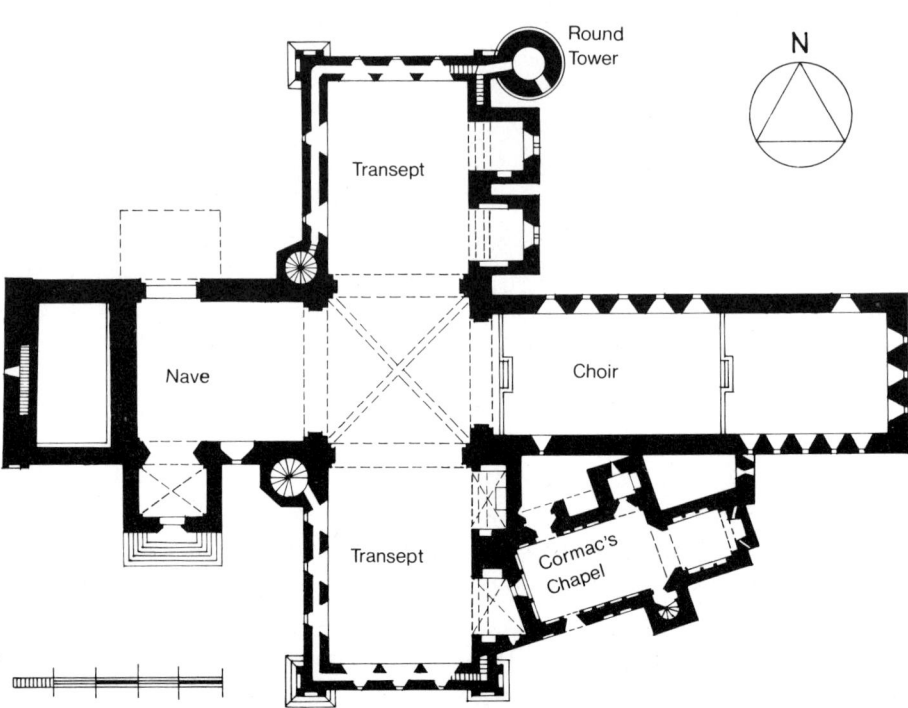

10 Cashel Cathedral

CATHEDRALS

CHAPTER 5

[Pl. 40] The Rock of Cashel seen from the north-east. At the bottom right is Hore Abbey established as a Cistercian monastery 1272.

they are quatrefoil in shape, inside they are given angle shafts and have segmental mouldings above and below. The need for such windows is hard to explain, for the lancets themselves would have flooded the interior with light; so probably they were a decorative feature, employed to fill a blank area of wall. With several choirs of similar design, this piece of individuality is refreshing to find.

[Pl. 41]
Cashel Cathedral, detail from north elevation of the choir (second quarter 13th century).

CHAPTER 5   CATHEDRALS

The refusal to conform is found elsewhere in the building. The crossing piers differ from each other as if the mason in charge attached no value to symmetry. And to show his exuberance, the bases of these piers are furnished with a double set of rolls, when one major roll was normal. The crossing and transepts are later than the choir, and the carving of the capitals takes on a different form. A combination of heads and foliage becomes the stock theme, a similar formula to that employed by the Gowran master. The Cashel work is coarse and stylised in comparison, though it is hard to tell how much this is the result of the hard limestone employed.

Outside, the transepts are decorated by a series of gabled niches, such as were once found in a similar position at St. Patrick's, Dublin. They were used on many English cathedrals of the period and it is worth noting that similar niches cover the facade of Wells Cathedral, which may be the ultimate source for Ireland [Pl. 35]. The nave of Cashel is remarkably short and apparently not built to its intended length. This halt in construction is ascribed to the financial troubles of Archbishop David MacCarwill (1253–89) who incurred heavy debts during his tenure of the see. Over a century later, the massive residential tower was built at the west end where the nave was no doubt once intended to go.

As a building constructed under Irish patronage, it is intriguing to compare Cashel with its Anglo-Norman neighbours. The similarity of the choir to New Ross shows that the Irish archbishops recruited masons who had previously worked on Anglo-Norman buildings in the area. But the oddities which appear at Cashel implies that they were less particular in their taste, or at least less familiar with architectural practice abroad. Whereas the archbishops of Dublin looked to England for their masons, the archbishops of Cashel were satisfied with more local craftsmen. Cashel was situated, however, in an area controlled by the Anglo-Normans so it was not surprising to find that the architecture is fundamentally alike. In areas like Connaught which were not under English control, the differences become more striking, but they are most noticeable in monastic architecture and are therefore left to the next chapter.

CHAPTER 5   CATHEDRALS

Ardfert Cathedral

The financial difficulties of Archbishop David MacCarwill remind us of the relative poverty of most of the Irish sees. The cathedrals so far discussed are exceptional in their size, and in many ways more typical is the cathedral at Ardfert on the coast of County Kerry [Pl. 42, Plan 11]. In the middle of the thirteenth century, the Romanesque church was replaced by one in the Gothic style. This is unusually long and originally it was unbroken by a transept, the present south transept being a fifteenth century addition. The choir is remarkable for its nine lancet windows in the south wall, treated almost as a decorative feature in their own right. Inside they have trefoiled rear arches forming a continuous arcade, dignified if slightly monotonous in character. Apart from three fine lancets at the east end, there is little else to break up the areas of blank wall, especially in the nave. This simple austere building was clearly erected with limited resources and it helps to show how lavish cathedrals like those in Dublin or Kilkenny must have appeared to the poorer Irish sees.

11 Ardfert Cathedral

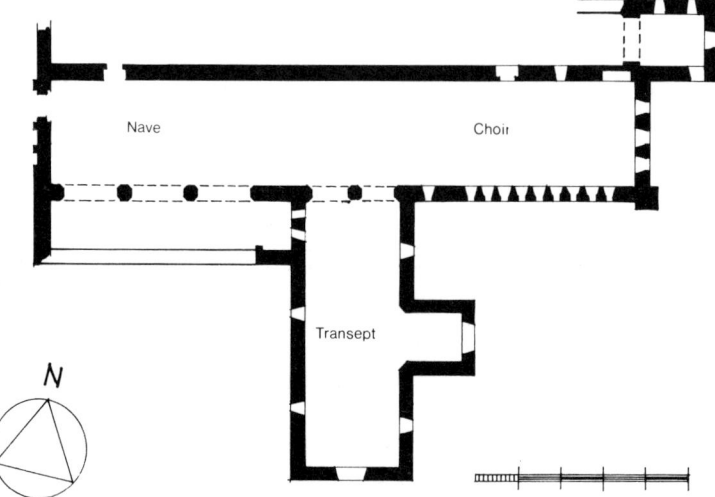

CATHEDRALS

CHAPTER 5

[Pl. 42]
St. Brendan's Cathedral, Ardfert,
the long aisleless choir seen from
the south-east (mid 13th century).

CHAPTER 6 ABBEYS AND FRIARIES

The Cistercians

The most important group of medieval churches in Ireland are those belonging to the Cistercian order, the monastic organisation which spread throughout Europe during the twelfth century. The order was founded in Burgundy in 1098 as a reaction to the excesses and luxury of many contemporary monasteries. Cistercian monks adopted a life of austerity and simplicity, dedicating themselves to poverty, labour, private prayer and contemplation. The first foundation in Ireland was Mellifont, dating from 1142, and eventually forty houses were established in the country.

Cistercian architecture was closely dictated by the ideals of the order. As the monks followed a life of simplicity, so their architecture had to be straightforward and free from non-essentials. Superfluous decoration was a dangerous luxury, a view cogently expressed by St. Bernard of Clairvaux, the most distinguished of the early Cistercians, when he wrote: 'works of art are idols, which turn men away from God and are at best of service to quicken the piety of weak souls and worldly persons'. The rules about ornament were sometimes loosely interpreted, as a look at such Irish houses as Boyle and Jerpoint soon shows. But for the most part the beauty of Cistercian buildings lies in the architecture itself, in its purity of form, in its sense of proportion, and in its skill of execution. Indeed the stonework—the precise cutting of the individual blocks—is one of the most admirable features, and it reaches a peak in the south arcade at Boyle [Pl. 49].

The order was more tightly organised than other monastic groups, each house being dependent on a mother abbey. Since every monastery followed the same rule of life, their architectural requirements were similar, with a need to incorporate several basic buildings—a church, a chapter house for meetings of the community, a dormitory, a refectory and kitchen as well as many subsidiary buildings. In the earliest abbeys in Burgundy a coherent scheme was evolved, a supremely rational piece of architectural planning. The various buildings were grouped around a central cloister [See Plan 13]. The church usually lay to the north, and the east range contained, among other rooms, the chapter house, with the monks' dormitory running along the first floor above. Then to the south came the refectory and kitchen, and along the west flank, the lay brothers' quarters.

ABBEYS AND FRIARIES — CHAPTER 6

The church itself was planned in an equally logical way. The presbytery was short, for the Cistercians placed no emphasis on rich liturgical ceremonies, and it usually ended square at the east. Private prayer and devotion required a number of smaller chapels, and these were neatly fitted against the east wall of the transept, the individual chapels roughly square in plan. The nave of the church was usually divided half-way by a screen, to separate the monks' choir from that of the lay brothers. The lives of these two classes of brethren were rigidly segregated. The lay brothers had living quarters of their own on the west side of the cloister, and their tasks were basically those of manual labour rather than reading or private contemplation. They frequently out-numbered the monks proper. At Jerpoint in 1227, out of a total community of eighty-six, fifty were said to be lay brothers.

The standard Cistercian plan as worked out in Burgundy was adopted in all the Irish houses, with only minor variations. Frequently the abbeys have more than their plan in common. The earliest houses of the order were constructed in the local Romanesque style of Burgundy, and certain features of this were carried by the Cistercians all over Europe. Of these, the pointed arch and the pointed barrel vault were the most important, and when they occur in Irish houses, as at Jerpoint and Boyle, they represent an ultimate debt to Burgundy [Pl. 47]. The pointed arch is usually associated with Gothic, but in Burgundy it had been employed prematurely as part of the Romanesque style.

But these are the only major debts which the Cistercian abbeys of Ireland owe to their foreign brethren. Their style is usually locally based, and it is noticeable that their buildings tend to fall into a series of regional groups. Occasionally as at Jerpoint and Baltinglass this is explained by the 'mother and daughter' relationship, elsewhere merely by geographical proximity, as in the case of Graiguenamanagh, Tintern and Dunbrody. So in Ireland there is no one Cistercian style of architecture. There are sometimes common features, and there is usually a common plan; otherwise there is plenty of variety to be found.

CHAPTER 6   ABBEYS AND FRIARIES

The advent of the Cistercian order occurred at a critical time from the point of view of style. During the second half of the twelfth century Romanesque, with its massive walls, its general use of the round arch and its distinctive range of ornament, was gradually replaced by the lighter, more elegant Gothic, characterised by the pointed arch. The Cistercians arrived in Ireland just before this transition occurred. Some of their earliest buildings are still fundamentally Romanesque, but their use of pointed arches and pointed barrel vaults gives them a transitional character. At Boyle a basically Romanesque design with cylindrical piers and round arches was used on the south arcade of the nave about 1180, but a few years later a Gothic scheme involving pointed arches and crocket capitals was employed on the corresponding arcade to the north. Other abbeys such as those at Grey Abbey and Inch [Pl. 3] were constructed throughout in an early Gothic style.

Mellifont

Unfortunately, it is hard to assess the exact development of Cistercian architecture in Ireland since the earliest church at Mellifont has been destroyed. Although its plan is known from excavation [Pl. 43, Plan 12], we remain ignorant about the rest of the design. As Mellifont was the parent house of many of the Irish abbeys, it could have exercised a crucial influence.

Mellifont's own mother house was Clairvaux in Burgundy. Since there were no previous Cistercian foundations in Ireland, St. Bernard, abbot of Clairvaux, sent over a certain Robert, who, the monks were told 'will advise you about how to further the buildings of the house and its other necessary requirements'. Robert presumably filled the rôle of architect, and he must have laid out the plan of the first church. Instead of the normal Cistercian scheme with square chapels in the transept he produced an unorthodox arrangement. In each arm of the transept there were three chapels, but whereas the two at the sides were furnished with apses the one in the middle ended square. The nearest parallels for this treatment are found in France, so it is a clear reflection of Robert's training abroad. As for the rest of his work at Mellifont, nothing is known.

ABBEYS AND FRIARIES

CHAPTER 6

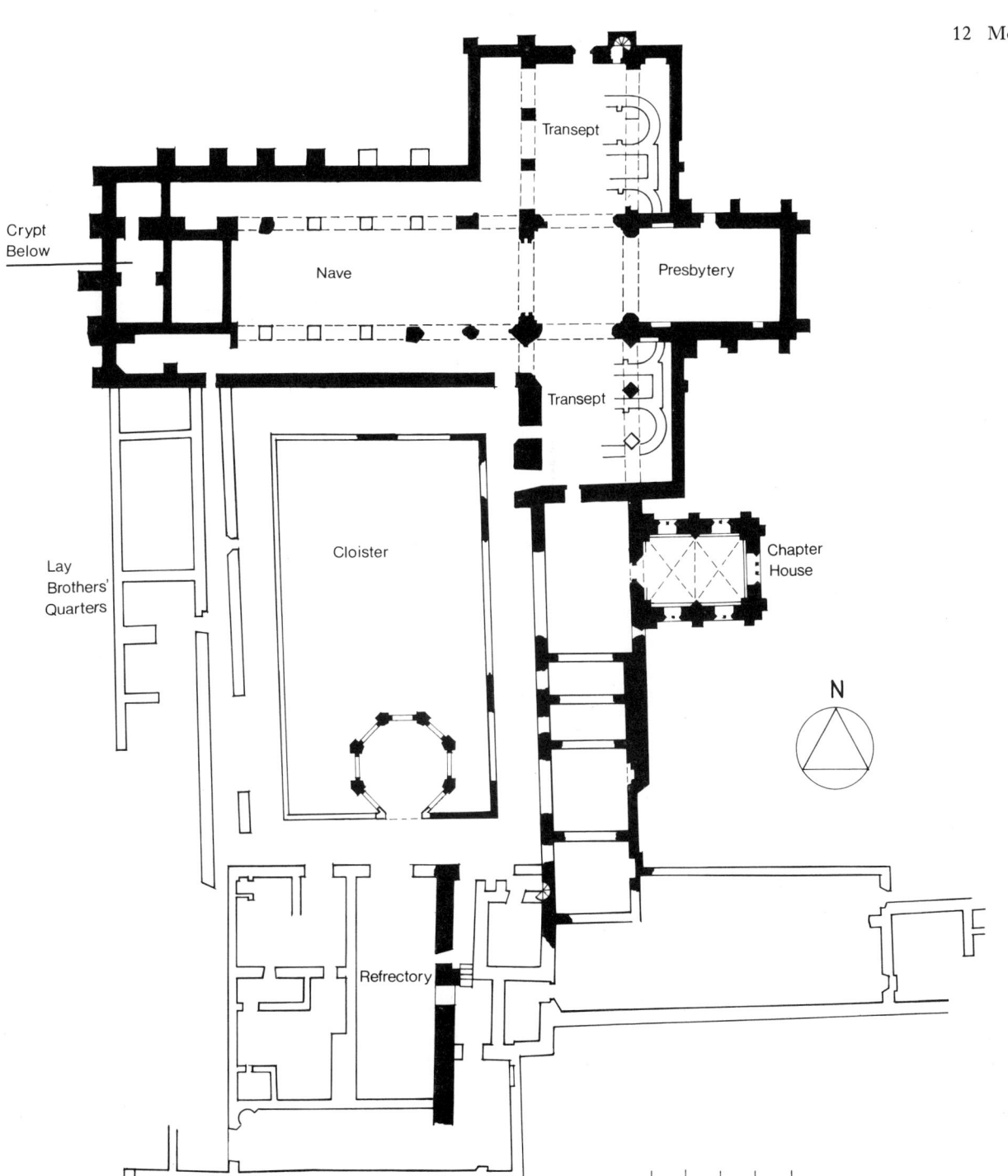

12 Mellifont Abbey

CHAPTER 6 ABBEYS AND FRIARIES

[Pl. 43]
Mellifont Abbey, view south across the transepts; the foundations of the chapels in the first church are visible in the centre foreground (c. 1142).

Already in the thirteenth century, this first church was reconstructed. Probably the architecture appeared too modest to accord with the abbey's claim to be the leading Cistercian house in Ireland, and a more grandiose church was required. Work began on the north transept and here the details are close to those in St. Patrick's, Dublin, a sign that the Cistercians were closely aware of the fashion of the day in non-monastic circles.

ABBEYS AND FRIARIES   CHAPTER 6

[Pl. 44]
Mellifont Abbey, lavabo (c. 1200) and cloister arcade.

But before the reconstruction of the church began the monks must have already built the magnificent lavabo, the only major building to survive partly intact, apart from the fourteenth century chapter house [Pl. 44]. Such an elaborate lavabo can scarcely have been a top priority building, which suggests that the abbey had money to spare by about 1200, the approximate date of construction: so by now the rest of the monastery must have been largely complete. Cistercian

[Pl. 45]
Mellifont Abbey, capital from the lavabo.

plumbing arrangements are always fascinating to trace. At Grey Abbey one of the main drains survives, and here at Mellifont we have the key point in the monastery's water supply. For a building with so mundane a function, the lavabo is a splendid piece of architecture. Octagonal in plan, a series of beautifully moulded arches opens into the main ground floor area. The shafts which support the arches have neatly carved capitals, decorated with stylised foliage designs [Pl. 45]. The use of the round arches suggests the Romanesque style, but the delicacy of the mouldings looks forward to Gothic, clear evidence that this is a transitional building.

ABBEYS AND FRIARIES CHAPTER 6

The ground floor was covered by a rib vault, and on the upper floor a water tank may have been situated. In the excavation of the cloister part of the lead feed-pipe from the adjoining river was discovered. No doubt further pipes led into fountains or basins on the ground floor to provide the monks with their washing facilities. These, it is worth noticing, were conveniently placed opposite the refectory entrance.

The lavabo must have been a mark of the abbey's prestige, for there was only one known parallel in Ireland, at Dunbrody, where it took a circular form. The Mellifont version may derive from its mother house at Clairvaux, which is known to have had one with a similar plan. Although found occasionally in other Cistercian houses, they must always have been a sign of affluence. The smaller abbeys of the order had to be content with basins in the cloister walk, fitted into the outside wall of the refectory. If the other buildings at Mellifont were as splendid as the lavabo, it must indeed have been a lavish monastery. The adjoining cloister arcades show greater restraint, however, for they rest on simple twin shafts and the capitals are no more than plain scallops.

Jerpoint

Better preserved than Mellifont is the abbey of Jerpoint, situated just south of Thomastown [Pl. 46, Plan 13]. Its foundation date is unknown but by 1180 it had become a daughter of Baltinglass, an abbey further north at the foot of the Wicklow Mountains. The architectural links between the two houses suggests that they were the product of the same directing mind, possibly one of the monks at Baltinglass. The design of the nave arcades is very similar in both places. Perhaps the most curious feature is the way the clerestory windows are sited over the piers, not over the arches as one would normally expect. This is copied in other Cistercian houses in Ireland, as in the south-eastern group of Graiguenamanagh, Tintern and Dunbrody [Pl. 60]. It is not easy to explain the purpose of the arrangement. It gives the design an interesting syncopated rhythm, but the explanation normally given is that it allowed a slight reduction in the height of the wall, though the saving is barely discernible at Jerpoint.

CHAPTER 6   ABBEYS AND FRIARIES

13 Jerpoint Abbey

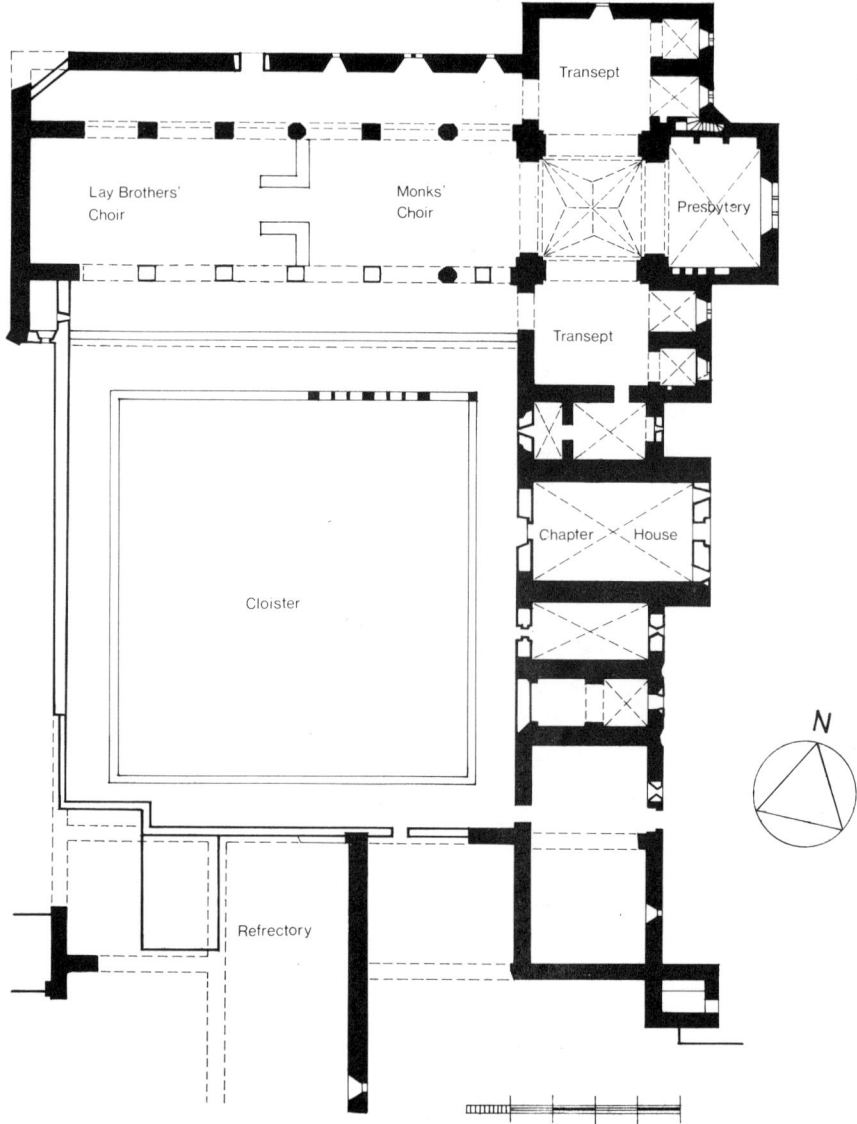

The piers of the nave arcade at Jerpoint also reveal a quest for variety. They start off at the east with alternating round and square forms, the same scheme as previously adopted at Baltinglass. Then half-way along comes a change. The final piers are polygonal in shape with columns fitted into the angles. Again the motive is hard to detect. It could be no more than a desire for variation, or possibly an attempt to look more up to date.

[Pl. 46] Jerpoint Abbey, the north arcade of the nave showing the changes in pier form (c. 1180–90).

CHAPTER 6 ABBEYS AND FRIARIES

The lower parts of the piers are disfigured by rough walls of masonry and this was part of the screen intended to keep the monk's choir strictly segregated from the rest of the church. But having erected an arcade of austere beauty, it seems strange that the monks ruined it with such a clumsy device. Again it is a feature that Jerpoint shares with Baltinglass, and these so-called perpyn walls also occur elsewhere. They are found at Boyle as well as in the Welsh abbeys of Buildwas and Strata Florida.

Boyle

Contemporary with Jerpoint though different in style is the abbey of Boyle, the finest of the Cistercian churches to survive in Ireland. It was described by Arthur Champneys, one of the pioneers of Irish architectural history, as the 'greatest offender against the simplicity of the Cistercian order', a reference to the amount of decorative carving contained in the church. The architecture itself is equally fine, and the majesty of the south arcade is unparalled elsewhere in the country.

The presbytery was the first part of the church to be built, soon after 1161 [Pl. 47, Plan 14]. It is covered by a plain pointed barrel vault, typical of early Cistercian architecture. In Ireland such vaults were usually restricted to the presbytery and chapels, the most precious and sacred part of the church, but presumably it was only cost that prevented their construction in the rest of the building, for they were an effective security against fire. The presbytery at Boyle is now lit by three striking early English lancets. These were inserted in the thirteenth century, and the original windows were considerably smaller. As first constructed, therefore, the presbytery would have been much darker.

Reaching the crossing there is a sudden contrast in scale. The round arches into the nave and transepts are several feet higher than the pointed arch into the presbytery, a difference which is partly concealed by the construction of a tower above. Although the details of the tower are later, it seems that it was planned from the start, in flagrant contravention of Cistercian rules. In 1157—only four years before

ABBEYS AND FRIARIES CHAPTER 6

the start of Boyle—the General Chapter had passed a regulation banning towers as an unnecessary luxury. The rule was frequently broken in England, but only occasionally in Ireland at this date, for most of the existing Irish towers are fifteenth century additions. If a tower was constructed as part of the original work at Boyle it was a further act of disobedience.

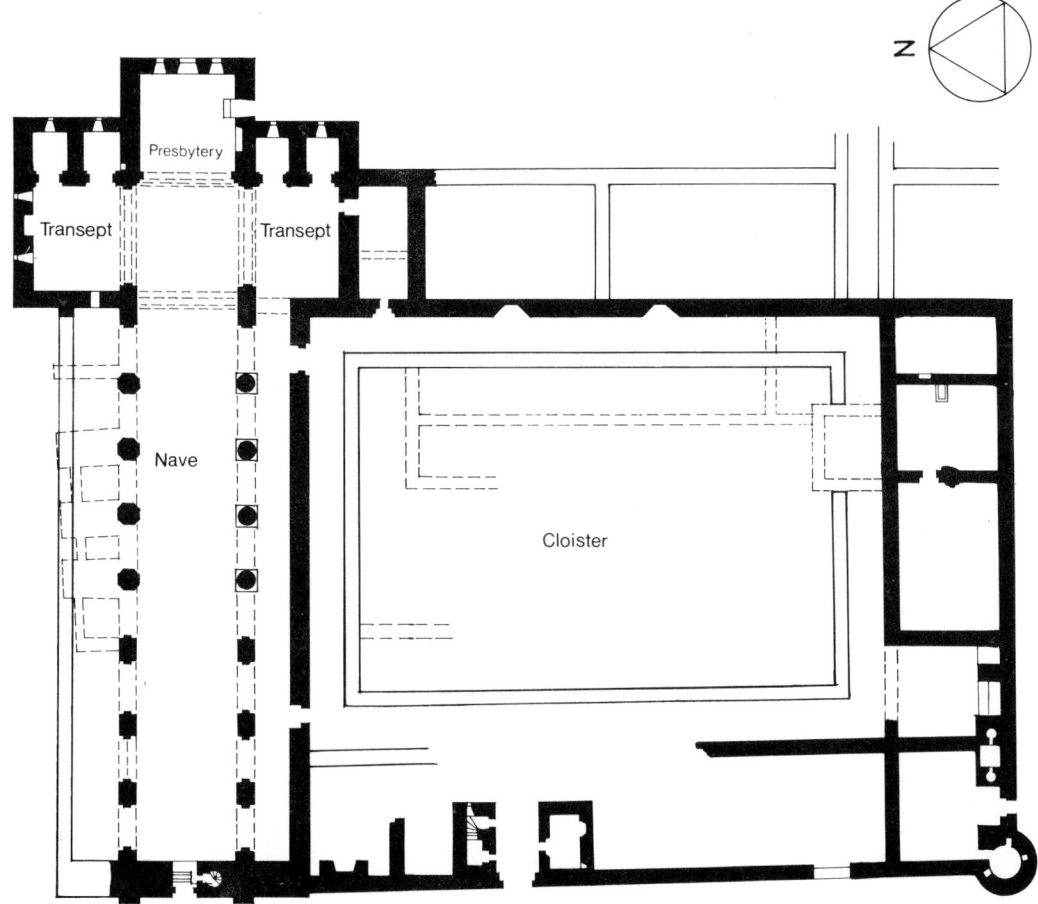

14 Boyle Abbey

[Pl. 47]
Boyle Abbey, presbytery (c. 1161).

[Pl. 48]
Abbey Knockmoy, detail of corbel (c. 1220).

Three of the arches below the tower rest on half columns against the wall, but the arch into the nave rests on corbels which gradually taper away. The use of such tapering corbels is a general characteristic of Cistercian architecture, both in Ireland and abroad. Originally the stalls of the monks were placed below, flush against the western piers of the crossing. Had the corbel been extended downwards as a half column, it would have caused a slight obstruction. The tops of the corbels are decorated with rope-like ornament, and in the neighbouring abbey of Knockmoy these were more lavishly treated [Pl.48]. The final taper of some is carved with a pattern of foliage, complete with an amusing twist at the bottom.

103

CHAPTER 6 ABBEYS AND FRIARIES

About 1180 work must have been begun on the nave. The eastern four arches on the south side were apparently built first, for they are earlier in style than the rest [Pl. 49]. The round arches are supported by imposing cylindrical piers, not unlike those found in several Cistercian abbeys in England. In the middle of the twelfth century similar arcades were erected at Buildwas on the Welsh border, and it appears that Boyle was derived from a model of this sort. The treatment is very different from Baltinglass and Jerpoint, where cylindrical piers were also employed. At Boyle, there is no alternation with piers of other shape, and the clerestory windows are sited in orthodox fashion over the arches. The origins of the design at Boyle, therefore, are not to be found in Ireland, unless the early church at Mellifont provided a prototype, but this we shall never know.

Although living in the west of Ireland remote from English influence, the monks at Boyle were remarkably well informed on architectural matters, though somewhat fickle in their taste. Instead of building the north arcade to match the southern one, a different and more advanced design was produced. The piers consist of clusters of small attached shafts [Pl. 50], and the arches themselves are pointed. It is hard to believe that this reflects a simple desire for variation, and it may be that some unknown disaster led to the arrangement. But more probably the monks were simply concerned to get the latest style, even at the cost of harmony. This was a grave problem when resources were limited and building slow, for the initial design quickly became old fashioned. Confronted with the problem of whether to continue in an outdated or a new style, the monks at Boyle opted for the latter.

The same problem arose some years later about 1210–20 at the west end of the nave [Pl. 51]. Here there is another dramatic break in design, though at least this time there was some attempt to keep the north and south arcades alike. The piers are basically square with a cluster of triple shafts on their inner faces. Triple shafts are a feature of English west country architecture just before the turn of the century. They appear at Wells and Glastonbury in the 1180's, they were employed in the choir of Christ Church, Dublin about the same time, and they are used conspicuously in the nave of Llandaff Cathedral on the coast of South Wales. Once again the work at Boyle

[Pl. 49]
Boyle Abbey, the south arcade
of the nave (c. 1180).

[Pl. 50]
Boyle Abbey, detail from pier on the north arcade of the nave (c. 1190–1200).

reflects a knowledge of architecture elsewhere. Had the abbey been an Anglo-Norman foundation, English connections might have been expected, but the abbey was predominantly Irish and the abbots of Boyle are known to have been Irishmen.

[Pl. 51]
Boyle Abbey, the west window and adjoining bay of the nave (c. 1220–30).

CHAPTER 6 ABBEYS AND FRIARIES

Any attempt to explain the frequent changes leads to the question of who drew up the designs. Practice elsewhere in Europe shows that it was common for a monk himself to be in control. At Walkenried in Germany, for example, the plan was provided by two monks, Jordan and Berthold, and the actual building done by twenty-one lay brothers, stone-cutters and masons under monastic supervision. At Boyle the monk Donnsleibhe O hInmhainén supervised the carpenters before 1230, and one wonders whether another monk supervised the masons. Yet outsiders as well were apparently employed at the abbey for some of the carving is done by craftsmen who worked in neighbouring non-Cistercian churches. The employment of outside labour was by no means abnormal and St. Bernard himself hired workmen in 1133 to help in the reconstruction of Clairvaux. The number of outside craftsmen almost certainly increased in the course of time. When the first Cistercian abbeys were founded in Ireland, relatively few skilled masons must have been available in the country, so the monks and lay brothers would have been forced to do the bulk of the work themselves. But, with the expansion of building after the Anglo-Norman invasion, the number of masons would have gradually increased, providing more opportunity for the Cistercians to recruit from outside. At Boyle the later work may well have been controlled by a professional mason, since the design reveals such a close knowledge of the latest architecture in the west of England. As already suggested the west window may even be the work of the Christ Church master. But the earliest work in the presbytery is so typically Cistercian that the monks were undoubtedly in control at this stage. The various transformations in style suggest, therefore, that as building moved forward, monastic control was replaced by the supervision of outside masons.

The sculptors of Boyle
Carving by several different hands can be detected in various parts of the church. In the nave many corbels and capitals are decorated with abstract foliage designs which are clearly the work of a local craftsman. The designs form a continuous and tightly-knit pattern and it is noticeable that the carving itself is very shallow. Although the sculptor was precise in his work, he rarely cut deeply into the stone. Some of

ABBEYS AND FRIARIES — CHAPTER 6

[Pl. 52]
Boyle Abbey, capital with trumpet scallops at the west end of the nave (c. 1220).

the capitals have trumpet scallops with the foliage pattern added above [Pl. 52]. The trumpet scallop was a favourite design in the western parts of Britain at the end of the twelfth century, so the capitals at Boyle illustrate the way in which one Irish craftsman adapted English motifs to his own needs. He must have been at work some time between 1200–20.

As well as carving the capitals required at the west end, he also produced a series of corbels which were fitted in the spandrels of the

109

CHAPTER 6　　　　　　　ABBEYS AND FRIARIES

arches throughout the nave [Pl. 49, 50]. The style of the carving and the profile of the abaci show that these were additions made at the time when the last three bays of the church were under construction. Their purpose is obscure. They are too low to support vaulting ribs, nor is the nave adequately buttressed to receive a vault. Similarly placed shafts and corbels can be found at St. David's Cathedral, South Wales, which was under construction at the same time. Here it seems they were intended to support wall posts which extended down from the wooden roof above. Those at Boyle may have served the same function. Further corbels were placed in the aisles of the nave, and here they may well have supported vaulting ribs, though none of the ribs themselves remain.

All the additional corbels were carved in the same workshop. Most of them have standard foliage patterns which formed the basic repertoire. At times more imagination is shown and a few of the capitals at Boyle are decorated with extravagant animals [Pl. 53]. There is one attempt to depict human figures, a strange group of men clutching the branches of trees [Pl. 54]. In this case the carving is crude and clumsy, and shows that the sculptor's limitations were exposed when he abandoned his favourite leaf and animal motifs.

Similar carvings are found at several other churches in the neighbourhood. Were these the work of the same craftsman and his companions? In every case the style is so close that one has little hesitation in attributing it to the same man, though no doubt he had his assistants. His foliage designs appear in the abbey of Knockmoy, founded in 1190 as a daughter house of Boyle, and a corbel there, decorated with leaves, has already been mentioned [Pl. 48]. It is not surprising to find craftsmen moving from one Cistercian abbey to another, but this particular group also worked outside the order at the three abbeys of Cong, Inishmaine and Ballintubber. At Cong the various doorways are embellished with a profuse quantity of foliage, and the designs at Inishmaine take a similar form. But in the choir of Ballintubber the work became more adventurous [Pl. 55, 56]. The abbey was founded in 1216, so we can safely date the sculpture in the church to the years around 1220. The carving is now more competent, the designs are more vigorous, and the cutting is far bolder. On many

ABBEYS AND FRIARIES

CHAPTER 6

[Pl. 53]
Boyle Abbey, capital at west end
of the nave (c. 1220).

CHAPTER 6 ABBEYS AND FRIARIES

[Pl. 54]
Boyle Abbey, capital at west end of the nave (c. 1220).

capitals wild beasts ferociously stare at each other, on others their bodies are violently inter-twined. This was just the type of ornament which had been anathema to St. Bernard, but as an Augustinian house, Ballintubber did not of course have to conform to Cistercian ideals of austerity.

ABBEYS AND FRIARIES

CHAPTER 6

[Pl. 55]
Ballintubber Abbey, capital in the choir (c. 1220).

CHAPTER 6 ABBEYS AND FRIARIES

[Pl. 56]
Ballintubber Abbey, capital in the
choir (c. 1220).

ABBEYS AND FRIARIES

CHAPTER 6

[Pl. 57] Ballintubber Abbey, carving on the east window (c. 1220).

CHAPTER 6 ABBEYS AND FRIARIES

The east windows of Ballintubber are more lavishly carved than their counterparts in Cistercian abbeys, and again the hand of the Boyle sculptor can be detected [Pl. 57]. Outside, his characteristic foliage appears, but inside he produced far more exciting work. The mouldings round the windows continue up to the base of the arch where one would expect a capital, but here two of the mouldings are developed into the heads of dragons, snarling at a bizarre face which lies between them. The dragons recall similar carving on a late Romanesque doorway at Killaloe Cathedral further south in county Clare, and the face, carved in a very shallow relief, is reminiscent of those in Tuam Cathedral, a few miles east of Ballintubber. This shows that the sculptor's style was rooted in the traditions of Irish Romanesque, for although working in a period normally regarded as Gothic, his work is essentially Romanesque; indeed he is one of the most distinguished of the Irish Romanesque sculptors.

These five churches in which he and his assistants worked were all in Connaught. Three of them were founded by members of the ruling O Conor family, and a fourth, Inishmaine, had an abbot who belonged to the royal dynasty. This was Maelisa O Conor who died in 1223, and it is likely that the Boyle sculptor worked at Inishmaine just before his death. This craftsman can thus be regarded as an artistic representative of the O Conor family. He does not appear to have worked for the Anglo-Normans. Similar carving can be found at other churches in the west of Ireland, notably at Corcomroe, Killaloe and Drumacoo, all founded under Irish patronage, and they may be further works of the Boyle sculptor or his companions.

Although his style was archaic by European standards, this does not detract from its interest in an Irish context. His sculpture may not be outstandingly beautiful. But it is honest and straightforward and provides an attractive form of ornament. The carving is frequently associated with a certain style of architecture, to which H. G. Leask gave the title 'the school of the west'. It is characterised by late forms of chevron ornament and by windows which have continuous mouldings unbroken by any capital [Pl. 58]. Apart from Boyle, at least one

ABBEYS AND FRIARIES

CHAPTER 6

[Pl. 58]
Ballintubber Abbey, east windows (c. 1220); late forms of chevron and continuous mouldings are characteristic of the school of the west.

of these characteristics appears in every church where the sculptor and his team worked, suggesting that both the architecture and the carving were their responsibility. However, further research is required before definite conclusions can be reached.

CHAPTER 6   ABBEYS AND FRIARIES

[Pl. 59]
Corcomroe Abbey (c. 1200); its isolation is typical of Cistercian monasteries.

Corcomroe

Although the sculpture of Boyle is closely related to local work, its architecture remained exceptional. More typical of Cistercian design in the west of Ireland is the abbey of Corcomroe [Pl. 59, Plan 15]. Its official name was 'Santa Maria de petra fertili'—St. Mary of the fertile rock—a title which reminds us of its isolated situation in the stony hills of county Clare. To be free from the distractions of secular life,

ABBEYS AND FRIARIES — CHAPTER 6

the Cistercians always searched for secluded places in which to build their abbeys, though the seclusion often diminished as time went by owing to the growth of towns and villages alongside. But Corcomroe retains much of its original isolation and gives a splendid idea of the remote places in which the Cistercians first lived.

The exact date of the abbey's foundation is not known, but it was some time between 1175 and 1195. It was never a wealthy abbey and consequently the buildings are small. The church, for example, has only one chapel in each transept. The arches of the nave have been partially blocked up, but it is still possible to make out the massive square piers and the plain pointed arches above [Pl. 59]. This severe style, which conformed to Cistercian ideals more closely than did the design of churches such as Boyle, is also found in the abbeys of Monasternenagh and Knockmoy, thus forming a regional group easily distinguished from others. All three were apparently Irish foundations.

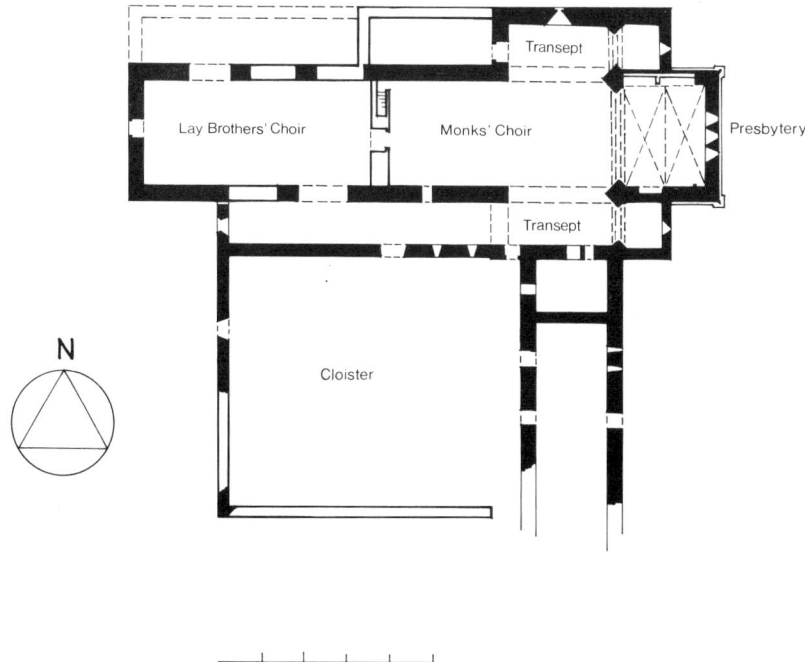

15 Corcomroe Abbey

CHAPTER 6 ABBEYS AND FRIARIES

Dunbrody

In comparison, the architecture of the south-eastern group of churches—Graiguenamanagh, Tintern and Dunbrody—appears extravagant, and significantly all were Anglo-Norman foundations. Delicate mouldings appear in the arcades, dog-tooth ornament abounds, and the general scale of the buildings is much greater, all of which reflects the more lavish endowment they received. The churches have one further detail in common. Most of the clerestory windows are designed as twin lancets, placed over the piers between the arches.

Dunbrody, the most attractive of the three and the least affected by subsequent reconstruction, lies in picturesque surroundings beside the estuary of the river Suir in county Wexford [Pl. 60, Plan 16]. The land was given to the Cistercians by Hervey de Montmorency, the uncle of Strongbow, in the years following the Anglo-Norman invasion. Originally his grant was made to the English abbey of Buildwas, and in 1182 the abbot sent a lay brother named Alan to inspect the site. He found the place completely desolate and was forced to use a hollow oak tree as his lodging while the boundaries of the land were being marked out. He presented an adverse report to his abbot, telling of the sterility of the land and the fierceness of the barbarous people living in the neighbourhood. Consequently the abbot of Buildwas made over his rights under Hervey's charter to St. Mary's, Dublin, and it was from there that Dunbrody was colonised. According to one of the early charters, the monks were soon busy in the place, erecting their buildings and 'converting the wilderness into a garden'. The information contained in the charters thus provides a rare description of the early establishment of an abbey.

Most of the existing ruins date from the first half of the thirteenth century. The plan of the church follows an orthodox Cistercian layout, with three chapels contained in the arm of each transept. The earliest work in the presbytery is austere, the windows no more than plain lancets with mouldings reduced to a minimum. But in the nave there is far more decorative work. The surviving twin window in the clerestory is especially well executed, with delicate mouldings running down behind the central shaft [Pl. 61]. The great west

ABBEYS AND FRIARIES CHAPTER 6

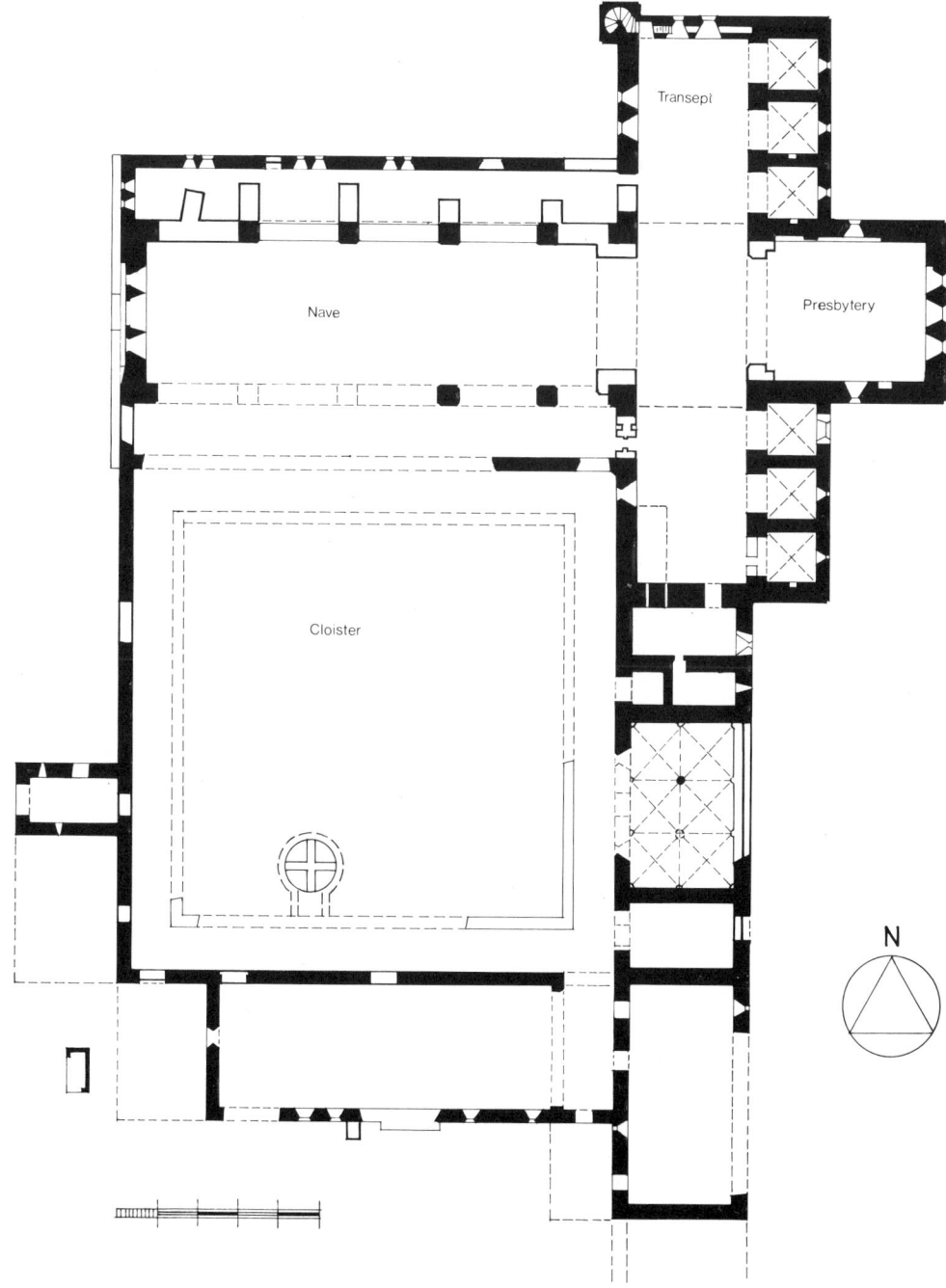

16 Dunbrody Abbey

CHAPTER 6 ABBEYS AND FRIARIES

[Pl. 60]
Dunbrody Abbey, the surviving north arcade of the nave (first half 13th century).

window has been destroyed, but an engraving of it was made in the eighteenth century [Pl. 62]. It consisted of three lancets with three circular motifs added above, and although it looks attractive in the engraving, the design was rather outdated by European standards. The technique employed is known as 'plate tracery', whereby the openings are cut through the wall leaving much bare masonry either side. By the middle of the thirteenth century this technique was being replaced by a more refined method known as 'bar tracery', whereby the main arch of a window was divided by slender bars of masonry with no part of the solid wall left. A comparison between

ABBEYS AND FRIARIES CHAPTER 6

[Pl. 61]
Dunbrody Abbey, detail of clerestory windows.

CHAPTER 6 ABBEYS AND FRIARIES

[Pl. 62]
Dunbrody Abbey, engraving of the west window (c. 1250) from Grose's 'Antiquities of Ireland'.

the Dunbrody window and the fourteenth century east window at Jerpoint will make the point clear [Pl. 72]. It seems that the masons employed at Dunbrody did not have sufficient skilled knowledge to embark on the new and more complicated technique.

Nevertheless the nave contains much fine craftsmanship. It is a pity that both the west window and the south arcade were allowed to fall within the last two hundred years, for when complete it must have been one of the finest Cistercian churches in Ireland. The differences between its architecture and that of abbeys like Corcomroe or Boyle are clearly apparent. Once again it illustrates the regional character of Irish Cistercian architecture.

ABBEYS AND FRIARIES CHAPTER 6

The Augustinian Canons

Cistercian houses were not the most numerous in Ireland, although their architecture overshadows that of other religious communities. The largest group were the Canons Regular of St. Augustine. Although they outnumbered the Cistercians, only thirty of their abbeys survive, of which about eight are reasonably large. The order had developed in the second half of the eleventh century, and it was introduced to Ireland by St. Malachy as part of his attempt to reform the Irish church. There were many foundations before the invasion of 1169, and about sixteen more were subsequently established by the Anglo-Normans.

The canons followed a rule derived from the writings of St. Augustine of Hippo, but this formed merely a basis: individual abbeys added their own liturgical uses and there was considerable variety among them. In Ireland many followed the rule practised in the Augustinian house at Arrouaise in northern France. The Augustinians were not therefore a coherent order like the Cistercians. They were largely independent of each other and their way of life often differed between communities. Some were founded in isolated places in the country and offered a strict semi-contemplative life, almost indistinguishable from that lived in Cistercian monasteries of the day. Others served the needs of cathedrals and this was often the case in Ireland. Both Christ Church, Dublin and Newtown Trim, for example, had communities of Augustinian canons. Inevitably this led to closer association with local people than was normal for the Cistercians, and as a result their architecture tends to be locally based. Moreover, just as there was no standard rule of life, so there was no standard architectural scheme. The style of Augustinian houses thus varies from one to another.

Athassel

The huge Augustinian priory of Athassel is perhaps the most exciting of all the Irish monastic sites [Pl. 63, Plan 17]. Founded by William de Burgh some time before 1205, the priory was constructed in a bend of the river Suir, and lies in a rich fertile valley, about a mile south of Golden in County Tipperary. This was one of the most important monasteries in Ireland and its buildings were extensive, as is shown in the aerial photograph. An outer wall originally surrounded the

CHAPTER 6 ABBEYS AND FRIARIES

[Pl. 63]
Athassel Priory, aerial view from the south; the gatehouse and bridge are situated towards the left; the church is on the far side of the monastic buildings.

priory and large parts of this remain. The main entrance was through an impressive gatehouse, in front of which is a bridge over a stream, now largely silted up. This stream was dug by the monastery and follows a straight course down from the main river at the top of the photograph. While adding to the defences of the priory, it was probably intended to drive a water mill.

ABBEYS AND FRIARIES

CHAPTER 6

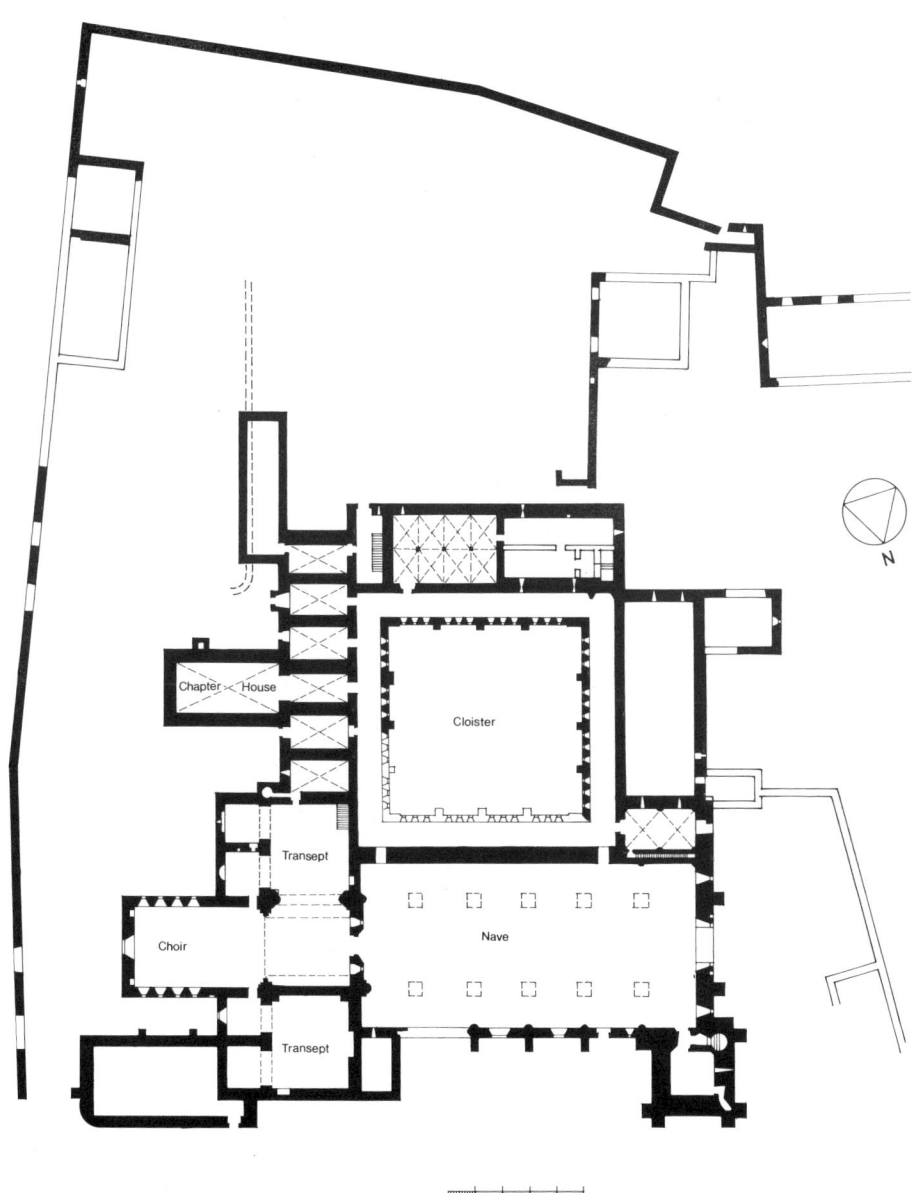

17 Athassel Priory

CHAPTER 6 ABBEYS AND FRIARIES

[Pl. 64]
Athassel Priory, the church from the north-west.

The church was built during the thirteenth century [Pl. 64]. The choir, lit by four tall lancet windows on each side, is similar to those in many Irish churches of the period. Unfortunately the architectural effect of the eastern parts of the building is now largely ruined by the walls which block up the arches of the transepts. There was always a central tower at this point, but it was rebuilt in the fifteenth century when these walls were added to strengthen it. Each arm of the transept was given two chapels and the way they are fitted into the design shows a clear debt to the Cistercians. Apart from the outer walls, the huge nave is destroyed. It was already derelict and roofless when the tower was built, for there is no roof creasing on its west wall. The loss of the nave at Athassel is a serious gap, for the design was almost certainly one of the most significant in Ireland at the period. Excavation is desperately needed, for the shape of the nave piers might well be discovered, and this would help to throw light on the design of the elevation above. Fragments of massive capitals survive, decorated with the fashionable stiff leaf. The aisles were apparently vaulted, for several of the wall shafts remain *in situ*. At the west end there was once a magnificent window, where one might have seen some elaborate tracery, all too rare in Ireland.

The nave itself was always divided from the choir by a screen wall, and a fine thirteenth century doorway opens through this [Pl. 65]. The arches are decorated with dog-tooth and once rested on detached shafts which have now disappeared. All this is very much in line with English work of the period. The capitals are carved with foliage, very stylised in appearance. Above the doorway is a huge arch, blocked when the tower was reconstructed in the fifteenth century. Originally this must have opened into a gallery beneath the tower, and here, above the doorway, a crucifix was probably placed, forming a climax to the view up the nave.

Many of the cloister buildings still survive to a great height, though most of them are covered by vegetation. The general layout is similar to that in Cistercian houses with a chapter house situated on the eastern side. Running at right-angles above the entrance to this, and above the adjacent chambers, was the dormitory where it is still possible to walk. Steps lead down into the south transept of the church, and these 'night stairs', as they are called, are also a prominent feature of Cistercian churches. They allowed the monks to come direct from the dormitory to say the nightly offices in the church.

Along the south wall of the cloister lie the ruins of the refectory. This was placed on the first floor above a vaulted basement. At the end of the west walk of the cloister is another elaborate thirteenth century doorway which provided an impressive entrance to the refectory above. Two other such doorways survive elsewhere in the priory.

CHAPTER 6 ABBEYS AND FRIARIES

[Pl. 65]
Athassel Priory,
doorway leading
into choir
(mid 13th century).

ABBEYS AND FRIARIES
CHAPTER 6

Ballintubber

Although Athassel was designed with more splendour than Cistercian abbeys, the plan of both the transepts and the eastern range of cloister buildings owes a great deal to Cistercian architecture. Cistercian influence is equally apparent at the Augustinian abbey of Ballintubber in county Mayo, the church in which the sculptor from Boyle was employed [Pl. 66, Plan 18]. As at Athassel, the plan is closely based on Cistercian schemes; so too are other features of the design. The choir has a rib vault, with individual ribs of plain square section, and this is similar to those erected in the neighbouring Cistercian abbeys of Knockmoy and Corcomroe. The ribs rest on triple shafts which taper into the wall, according to Cistercian practice. At a time when there were few other major churches in Connaught, it was natural for Ballintubber to look to its Cistercian neighbours and copy their methods, and it helps to demonstrate the importance of the Cistercian contribution to Irish architecture.

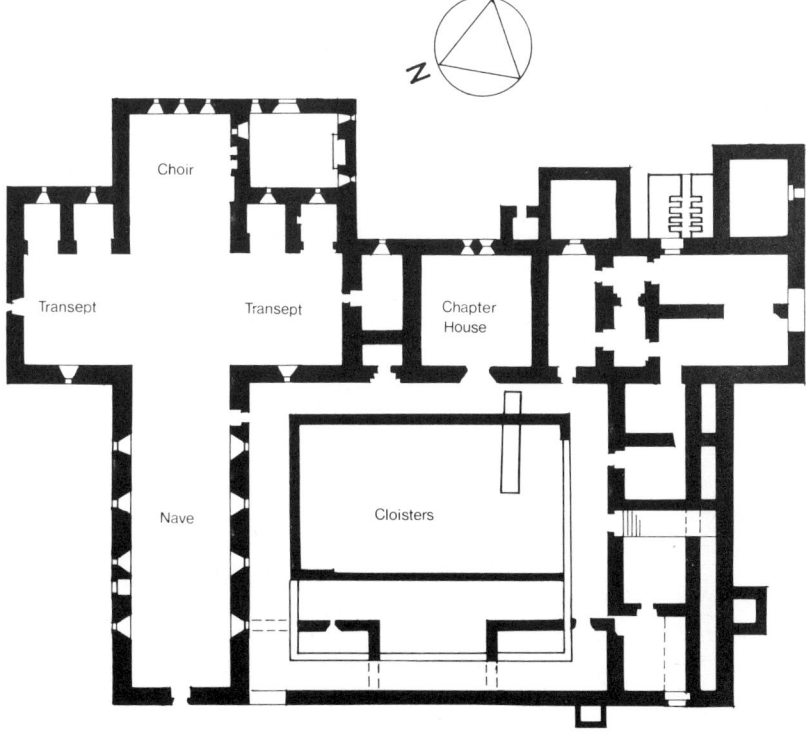

18   Ballintubber Abbey

[Pl. 66] Ballintubber Abbey, the choir (c. 1220).

ABBEYS AND FRIARIES — CHAPTER 6

Few Irish monasteries survived the dissolutions of the sixteenth century and over the last four hundred years the majority have deteriorated into ruins, many vanishing completely. The church at Ballintubber, however, was recently restored with great care, and it provides a convincing impression of a church interior in Ireland during the early decades of the thirteenth century.

The Friars

Apart from the Cistercians and Augustinians, the other religious orders which made a permanent impact on Irish architecture were the mendicants—the Dominican and Franciscan Friars. The Dominicans arrived in Ireland in 1224, less than twenty years after their founder, Dominic Guzman, had first preached in Languedoc against the Albigensian heresy. Preaching the Christian truths remained the *raison d'être* of the order. The Franciscans on the other hand came to Ireland a few years later, probably in 1231-2. They laid greater stress on material poverty than the Dominicans, following the example set by St. Francis of Assisi, and they tried to imitate as far as possible the way of life which Christ had lived on earth.

Both orders were thus committed to lives of poverty and humility, which allowed little opportunity for magnificent architecture. Their early churches were extremely simple. It was said that the Dominican church erected in Cambridge in 1238 was no more than the day's work of a single carpenter. Gradually, however, this stress on absolute simplicity was relaxed and by the early years of the fourteenth century both orders were constructing churches of considerable size. These were usually divided into two distinct parts. The choir, intended for the friars themselves, was clearly separated from the nave, which was intended for the layfolk. The central division was frequently stressed by a tower, and these are a striking feature of friary architecture in Ireland. When the nave became too small to house the congregations, aisles were added on the side away from the cloister, and often a spacious transept was constructed as well [see Plan 19]. These gave the churches a lop-sided effect, as the transepts could not be repeated on the opposite side, owing to the prior erection of domestic buildings.

CHAPTER 6   ABBEYS AND FRIARIES

Since an important part of the friars' lives involved ministering to the needs of the local community, their churches were constructed in towns and cities. In Britain the urban expansion of later centuries has destroyed a high proportion of them, but in Ireland many are better preserved. The finest medieval friaries to survive in the country date from the revival in the fifteenth century, when many were built in more isolated places. Nevertheless there is an important group of churches which date from an earlier period.

Kilmallock

The Dominican priory at Kilmallock illustrates some of the characteristics of friary architecture [Pl. 67, Plan 19]. It lies beside the river Loobagh just outside the town, once the capital of the Earls of Desmond. The Dominicans acquired the site in 1291 and the choir of the church must date from about the turn of the century. On

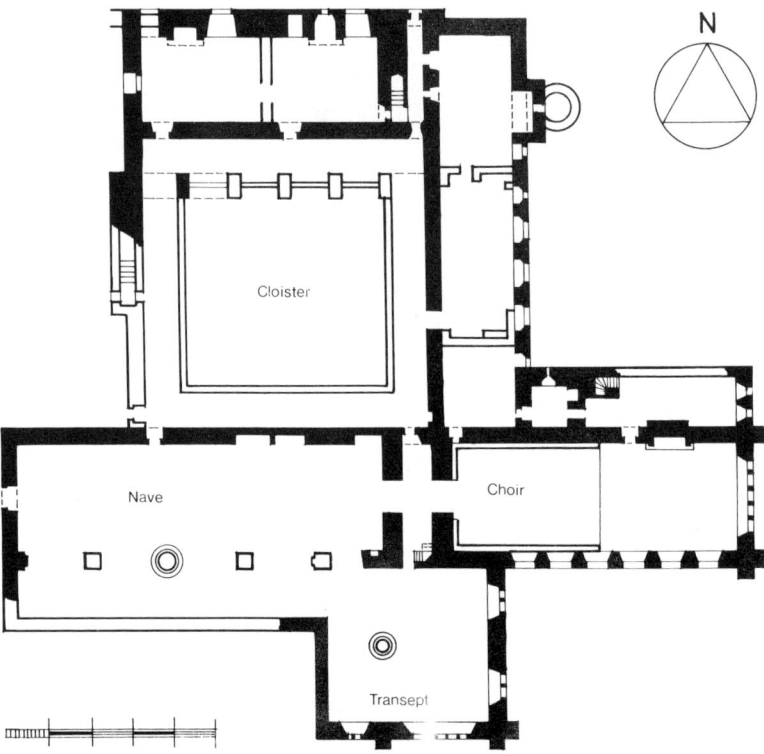

19 Kilmallock Priory

ABBEYS AND FRIARIES CHAPTER 6

[Pl. 67]
Kilmallock Priory,
the choir (c. 1300).

CHAPTER 6   ABBEYS AND FRIARIES

either side it has a magnificent enfilade of windows, the tracery now broken. A similar row exists in the Franciscan Friary at Ennis which dates from much the same period. The east window at Kilmallock has five graduated lancets with only slender mullions of masonry separating one from the other. The design is far more elegant than earlier work in Ireland, and in comparison lancets such as those at New Ross appear clumsy [Pl. 38].

The tower at Kilmallock was heightened at a later period, but it must have been started soon after the choir. A tall narrow arch leads through to the nave which has an aisle on the south side. Some time in the first half of the fourteenth century the transept was added, though the spectacular window in the south wall may be an insert of a hundred years later. On the east wall of the transept is a delicately carved niche, the main arch having a pointed trefoil head [Pl. 68]. The spandrels of the trefoil are embellished with leaves, carved in a naturalistic way, following a fashion which had become widespread in England by this time; it is a refreshing change from the stylised and rather monotonous work of the previous century. The line of the arch is decorated with ball flower ornament which was extravagently used at this period in England, though it is rare in Ireland. The capitals take the form of paired heads, but the carving is hard and lifeless, features which sadly become all too common in Irish sculpture of this time.

The cloister buildings are remarkably well preserved [Pl. 69], and although most of them have undergone subsequent reconstruction, some of the windows, which look out over the fields to the north, must date from the fourteenth century. The layout of the buildings is totally different from those of the Cistercians, and the plan of the church owes nothing to them either. The friars had their own particular requirements and their architecture was designed accordingly.

Kilmallock has taken us well into the fourteenth century, by which time the amount of building work in Ireland had begun to decline. There are several reasons for this but a discussion of them is better left to the next chapter.

[Pl. 68]
Kilmallock Priory, niche in the transept (first half 14th century).

CHAPTER 6 ABBEYS AND FRIARIES

[Pl. 69]
Kilmallock Priory, domestic buildings on the north side.

YEARS OF DECLINE

CHAPTER 7

The early fourteenth century

The invasion of Ireland by Edward Bruce between 1315 and 1318 is usually regarded as a turning point in the fortunes of the Anglo-Norman colony. It also marks the beginning of a lean period in Irish architecture. From a climax during the thirteenth century when building activity was intense, the number of new architectural projects now diminished appreciably. In part this reflects a decline in the number of new religious foundations. Hore Abbey, established in 1272 [Pl. 40], was the last of the medieval Cistercian houses, and subsequently the order carried out few major works until the fifteenth century. Instead the monks concentrated on relatively minor improvements, as at Jerpoint where a tracery window was constructed in the presbytery. Mellifont, the mother house of the order, was one of the few to undertake major alterations, for both the church and the chapter house were under reconstruction during the course of the century. The windows of the chapter house (visible in the background of Plate 43) have curvilinear tracery, and the doorway, unhappily destroyed in the eighteenth century, is known from an engraving which shows marble columns supporting an arch embellished with a mesh of carved foliage. The bulk of architectural work in the early fourteenth century, however, comes from the friars who continued to expand in the towns and cities of Ireland, their buildings becoming increasingly ambitious. Often they received substantial endowments which enabled them to embark on elaborate projects.

Castledermot

This was the case at the Franciscan friary of Castledermot which received a substantial endowment in 1302 from Thomas, Lord of Ossory. The friars already had buildings before this, since the house is mentioned in 1247. The plainest parts of the church, particularly the nave, must have been constructed about this time, but early in the fourteenth century the choir was lengthened and a magnificent transept was built to the north [Pl. 70, Plan 20]. These works were almost certainly financed by the grant of 1302.

The chief interest of the new buildings lies in the tracery of the windows, which give an indication of Irish window design at the period. The chapels in the transept were filled with 'switch line' tracery, in which the vertical mullions of the window divide near the

CHAPTER 7   YEARS OF DECLINE

top and curve away, those in the centre crossing each other. It forms an effective and simple pattern on small windows, but when used on a large scale as at the Black Abbey of Adare the design becomes repetitive and monotonous. It became a standard type, because it was easy to design and construct. The north wall of the transept at Castledermot was once filled with a rather curious elaboration of the scheme, and engravings of it survive [Pl. 71]. It consisted basically of switch line tracery, with a geometrical motif in the apex of the arch, a motif very weird in shape, if the engraving is to be believed. Indeed the work at Castledermot is a strange mixture of proficiency and incompetence. The mouldings of the arches and the switch line windows are well executed, but the northern chapel is curiously wider than the others as if the plan was not thoroughly worked out at the start, and the north window is by no means a beautiful design.

20 Castledermot Friary

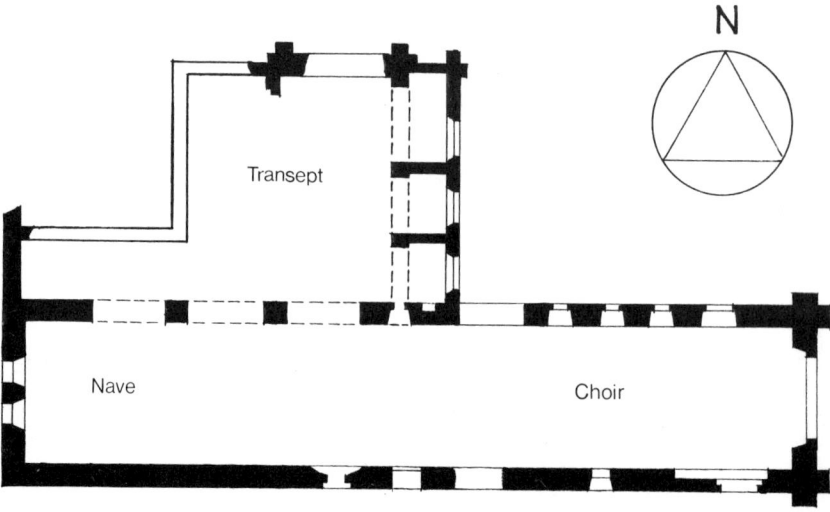

[Pl. 70] Castledermot Friary, north transept (c. 1302).

Dearth of skilled craftsmen

Despite the innovations in window construction, the more simple lancet forms continued in use well into the fourteenth century. The east window of the choir of the Franciscan friary in Kilkenny, constructed between 1321 and 1323, has no less than seven lancets grouped together in one composition. Although splendid in effect, it is interesting that a more advanced tracery pattern was not employed. Whether the lancets represent the aesthetic preference of the friars or whether they were limited by finance is hard to say, but it is also worth remembering that tracery required very exact cutting of the stone and demanded considerable geometrical knowledge from the master mason at the design stage. Since the amount of major architectural work available in Ireland was limited at this time, masons with the necessary skill must have been scarce. Indeed the quantity of building appears to have been insufficient to maintain a series of flourishing workshops like those existing in the previous century. The Black Death of 1348–9 must have accentuated the problem, for the plague no doubt reduced the number of skilled craftsmen. Perhaps this explains the uninspired design of the new choir at Christ Church, Dublin, erected through the munificence of Arch-

CHAPTER 7 YEARS OF DECLINE

[Pl. 71]
Castledermot Friary, engraving of north transept window from Grose's 'Antiquities of Ireland'.

bishop John of St. Paul after 1349 and demolished in the last century. Engravings show that the choir was lower in height than the earlier nave and that the windows contained merely switch line tracery, when here was an opportunity to produce something more ambitious. Whereas the design of the nave over a hundred years before reflected recent architectural thought in the west of England, the new choir bore no comparison to contemporary developments elsewhere. By this time there is no evidence of the transfer of masons from England to Ireland, and nowhere in the country are there any great works in the 'Decorated' or 'Perpendicular' style to compare with the 'early English' designs of Christ Church and St. Patrick's.

YEARS OF DECLINE CHAPTER 7

Window tracery

Tracery patterns at this time were becoming increasingly complex and they progressed from purely geometrical designs to the more flowing type of patterns commonly known as curvilinear. In Ireland the east window of the aisle at Gowran (c. 1260) represents an early form of the geometrical type, with trefoiled arches and a quatrefoil in the spandrel above [Pl. 37]. A more elaborate pattern was once found in the east window at Jerpoint [Pl. 72], inserted during the first half of the fourteenth century, a date suggested by the ball flower ornament in the arch. Unfortunately the filling of the oculus has been destroyed, but it seems to have had a curvilinear pattern with circular cusps like those in the three arches below. Two of these arches were elongated to fill the gap between the oculus and the wall, but the mason in charge evidently did not give sufficient prior thought to the design, for the heads of the arches had to be pushed out of the vertical. Either side of the window are the remains of two of its Romanesque predecessors, both carved with continuous chevron ornament. Some of the finest and most complicated tracery of the period in Ireland can be found at the two Dominican friaries of Kilkenny and Athenry [Pl. 73], where the craftsmanship is excellent, without any sign of the inexperience suggested at Castledermot and Jerpoint. Many equally fine windows have no doubt been destroyed, for tracery is particularly vulnerable to the ravages of time. One such loss is the east window at Tintern, originally filled with geometrical patterns which may well have reflected the spectacular tracery of its mother house in England, Tintern major, where the church was reconstructed from 1270 to 1301. But in Ireland the great period of tracery design was not to come until the fifteenth century.

Wars and plague

The effect of the Black Death and the plagues which followed are hard to determine precisely, for already the political and economic troubles of the early fourteenth century had made their impact on architecture. The devastations of the Scots between 1315 and 1318 and subsequent local wars reduced the profits from land, and thereby often reduced the surplus available for building. In 1334 the priory of Selskar in county Wexford alleged that all its lands and rents were destroyed by the war of the McMurhuth and other Irish, and other monastic houses evidently suffered similarly from the disturbances

[Pl. 72]
Jerpoint Abbey, east window (first half 14th century).

[Pl. 73]
Athenry Friary, window in the north transept (second quarter 14th century).

[Pl. 74]
St. Francis, Kilkenny, corbel beneath the tower (c. 1347).

[Pl. 75]
St. Francis, Kilkenny, corbel beneath the tower (c. 1347).

CHAPTER 7 YEARS OF DECLINE

of the time. Then on top of this came the plague. In 1351 the dean and chapter of Cashel said that their lands and rents had been 'all but totally destroyed by the king's Irish enemies and by the mortality of their tenants in the last plague'. The sterility of Irish architecture in the mid-fourteenth century therefore comes as no surprise.

Kilkenny Franciscan Friary

When the Black Death reached Ireland, the Franciscan friars of Kilkenny, having finished the extension of their choir, had embarked on new projects. In 1347 a confraternity was formed for 'erecting a new campanile and repairing the church', but work cannot have progressed far by the time the Black Death arrived in the town in 1349. The style of the windows in the upper parts of the tower suggest it remained unfinished for some time. The arches of the tower are supported on corbels which take the form of small 'atlas' figures [Pl. 74, 75]. The carving is rudimentary, again illustrating the dearth of highly skilled craftsmen, but the mason in his carving of one face has managed to produce a poignant expression of despair, an emotion which must have been only too prevalent at the time. The sculpture of these figures thus forms an appropriate symbol of the end of an epoch in Irish architecture and sculpture.